OECD Employment and Skills Strategies in Slovenia

This work is published under the responsibility of the Secretary-General of the OECD. The opinions expressed and arguments employed herein do not necessarily reflect the official views of OECD member countries, of ADB or its Board of Directors or the governments they represent.

This document and any map included herein are without prejudice to the status of or sovereignty over any territory, to the delimitation of international frontiers and boundaries and to the name of any territory, city or area.

Please cite this publication as:
OECD (2017), *OECD Employment and Skills Strategies in Slovenia*, OECD Publishing, Paris.
http://dx.doi.org/10.1787/9789264278929-en

ISBN 978-92-64-27891-2 (print)
ISBN 978-92-64-27892-9 (PDF)
ISBN 978-92-64-27898-1 (epub)

ISSN 2311-2328 (print)
ISSN 2311-2336 (PDF)

The statistical data for Israel are supplied by and under the responsibility of the relevant Israeli authorities. The use of such data by the OECD is without prejudice to the status of the Golan Heights, East Jerusalem and Israeli settlements in the West Bank under the terms of international law.

Photo credits: ©

Corrigenda to OECD publications may be found on line at: *www.oecd.org/about/publishing/corrigenda.htm*.
© OECD 2017

You can copy, download or print OECD content for your own use, and you can include excerpts from OECD publications, databases and multimedia products in your own documents, presentations, blogs, websites and teaching materials, provided that suitable acknowledgment of the source and copyright owner is given. All requests for public or commercial use and translation rights should be submitted to *rights@oecd.org*. Requests for permission to photocopy portions of this material for public or commercial use shall be addressed directly to the Copyright Clearance Center (CCC) at *info@copyright.com* or the Centre français d'exploitation du droit de copie (CFC) at *contact@cfcopies.com*.

Preface

While Slovenia was severely hit by the global financial crisis, the government responded with a number of reforms aimed at supporting domestic growth and demand. Labour market conditions are improving and the economic recovery that started to take effect in 2014 has helped to bring unemployment down to 8.0% in 2016 from a peak of 10% in 2013. However, vulnerabilities remain in the labour market, particularly in view of the low participation rate of older workers and the prevalence of skills shortages and mismatches in certain occupations. For these reasons, implementing effective employment and skills strategies at the local level is key to stimulate inclusive growth and generate more and better quality jobs for all Slovenians.

Over recent years, the work of the OECD LEED Programme on *Designing Local Skills Strategies, Building Flexibility and Accountability into Local Employment Services, Breaking out of Policy Silos, Leveraging Training and Skills Development in SMEs,* and *Skills for Competitiveness* has demonstrated that local strategies to boost skills and job creation require the participation of many different actors across employment, training, economic development, and social welfare portfolios. Employers, unions and the non-profit sector are also key partners in ensuring that education and training programmes provide the skills needed in the labour markets of today and the future.

The series of *OECD Reviews on Local Job Creation* deliver evidence-based and practical recommendations on how to better support employment and economic development at the local level. This report on Slovenia takes a case study approach, analysing the management and implementation of policies in the Drava and South-East regions of Slovenia. It provides a comparative framework to understand the role of local labour market policy in matching people to jobs, engaging employers in skills development activities, as well as fostering new growth and economic development opportunities. It includes practical policy examples of actions taken in Slovenia to help workers find better quality jobs, while also stimulating productivity and inclusion.

Going forward, the government should seek opportunities to work closer with employers to strengthen their ownership of the employment and skills development system. Public procurement policies, targeted financing mechanisms (e.g. training subsidies and tax credits) as well as local anchor institutions can play an important role in encouraging employers to adopt high-performance workplace practices and create incremental innovation within a local economy. It is also important to better join-up activities to promote better quality jobs. Local public employment services in Slovenia can play a stronger role in coordinating programmes among training providers and economic development agencies. The Slovenian Ministry of Labour, Family, Social Affairs and Equal Opportunities and the Government Office for Development and European Cohesion Policy should be warmly thanked for their active participation and support of the study, and for their ongoing partnerships with the OECD.

Foreword

This report was prepared as part of the Local Economic and Employment Development (LEED) Programme within the Centre for Entrepreneurship, SMEs, Local Development, and Tourism (CFE) of the Organisation for Economic Co-operation and Development (OECD). It has been undertaken in co-operation with the Slovenian Ministry of Labour, Family, Social Affairs and Equal Opportunities. Special thanks should be given to Ms Urška Kovač-Zlobko, within this Ministry as well as Mr Gorazd Jenko within the Government Office for Development and EU Cohesion Policy for their contributions to this report and participation in the OECD study visits.

Special thanks are also due to the local stakeholders in each of the case study areas of Drava and South-East Slovenia who participated in meetings and provided documentation and comments critical to this project.

This project has been coordinated by Jonathan Barr (Head of the Employment and Skills Unit), who was also one of the principal authors of this report, under the direction of Sylvain Giguère, Head of the LEED Division. The other principal authors are Tjaša Redek (University of Ljubljana) and Anna Rubin (OECD). Michela Meghnagi (OECD) and Pierre Georgin (OECD) provided valuable statistical and data analysis support. Thanks also go to François Iglesias (OECD) for production assistance and Janine Treves (OECD) and Angela Attrey (OECD) for useful editorial support.

Table of contents

Acronyms and abbreviations 8
Executive summary 9
Reader's guide 12

Chapter 1. **Policy context for employment and skills in Slovenia** 15
 Economic and labour market trends 16
 Education and skills 18
 National policy context: Increasing competitiveness and growth 20
 Employment policies and programmes 22
 Employment Services 24
 Vocational education and training policies 26
 Economic development and regional governance 27
 Note 29
 References 29

Chapter 2. **Overview of the Slovenian case study areas** 33
 Overview of the Drava and South-East Slovenia regions 34
 Balance between skills supply and demand at the sub-national level 39
 References 41

Chapter 3. **Local Job Creation dashboard findings in Slovenia** 43
 Theme 1: Better aligning policy and programmes to local economic development .. 45
 Theme 2: Adding value through skills 53
 Theme 3: Targeting policy to local employment sectors and investing in quality jobs 63
 Theme 4: Being inclusive 68
 References 76

Chapter 4. **Towards an action plan for jobs in Slovenia: Recommendations and best practices** 79
 Better aligning programmes and policies to local economic development 80
 Adding value through skills 84
 Targeting policy to local employment sectors and investing in quality jobs ... 89
 Being inclusive 91
 References 92

Tables
 1.1. Indicators for Main Goals 26
 2.1. Overview of the case study regions 37

3.1. Number of unemployed in Slovenia, case-loads per counselling personnel .. 48
3.2. PES collaboration with other stakeholders. 50
3.3. Overview of parental rights 72
3.4. Overview of Youth Guarantee pathway to employment 73

Figures

1.1. Growth rates of key economic indicators (%), 2000-15. 16
1.2. Unemployment rate across OECD countries, aged 15-64, 2015. 17
1.3. Youth unemployment rate (15-24) across OECD countries, 2015 18
1.4. Share of the population by educational attainment, aged 25-64, 2015 19
1.5. Mean literacy and numeracy scores, OECD Survey of Adult Skills (PIAAC), selected OECD countries and OECD average 20
1.6. Geographical organisations of the Employment Services of Slovenia (ESS) and NUTS3 statistical regions 25
1.7. Public expenditure on active and passive labour market measures (LMP) as a percentage of GDP, 2014 25
1.8. Slovenian regions. 28
1.9. Unemployment rate by region, 2008 and 2015. 29
1.10. Index of gross average monthly earnings by region (Slovenia = 100), 2015. . . . 29
2.1. GDP per capita index, Slovenian regions (Slovenia = 100), 2015 34
2.2. Regional GDP annual average growth rate, 2001-07 and 2008-14 36
2.3. Registered unemployment in selected regions 38
2.4. Unemployment rate by age groups, selected Slovenian regions, 2010 and 2015 38
2.5. Educational structure of employed by region, 2005-15. 38
2.6. Understanding the relationship between skills supply and demand 39
2.7. Balancing Skills Supply and Demand in Slovenia, 2013. 40
2.8. Balance of Skills Supply and Demand in Slovenia, 2013 41
3.1. Local job creation dashboard results for Slovenia. 44
3.2. Dashboard results for better aligning policy and programmes to local economic development. 45
3.3. Regional and local barriers to Public Employment Services (PES) performance improvements. 47
3.4. Dashboard results for adding value through skills 53
3.5. Participation rate in education and training (previous 4 weeks), aged 18-64, 2015. 56
3.6. Skills that the candidates are missing according to local employers, 2015. . . . 57
3.7. The responsiveness of Public Employment Services to local employer needs. . . . 58
3.8. Public expenditure on active labour market programmes (as % or GDP), 2013 . . . 61
3.9. Dashboard results for targeting policy to local employment sectors and investing in quality jobs 63
3.10. Dashboard results for being inclusive. 68
3.11. Share of Youth Not in Education, Employment or Training (NEET), age group 15-24, 2015. 73
3.12. Immigration to Slovenia: number of immigrants, 1990-2015 75

Follow OECD Publications on:

 http://twitter.com/OECD_Pubs
 http://www.facebook.com/OECDPublications
 http://www.linkedin.com/groups/OECD-Publications-4645871
 http://www.youtube.com/oecdilibrary
 http://www.oecd.org/oecddirect/

Acronyms and abbreviations

ALMP	Active Labour Market Policy
CPI	Center RS za Poklicno Izobraževalnih [Institute of the Republic of Slovenia for Vocational Education and Training]
CVET	Continuing Vocational Education Training
ESS	Employment Service of the Republic of Slovenia
FDI	Foreign Direct Investment
IMAD	Institute for Economic Research and Development
LMP	Labour Market Policy
MIC	Medpodjetniški Izobraževalni Centre [Inter-company training centres]
NEET	Not in Employment Education or Training
NUTS	Nomenclature of Territorial Units for Statistics
NVQ	National Vocational Qualifications
PES	Public Employment Service
SIAE	Slovenian Institute for Adult Education
SME	Small and Medium sized Enterprises
SORS	Statistical office of the Republic of Slovenia
VET	Vocational Education and Training

Executive summary

Relative to other OECD countries, Slovenia compares well on most economic, education and social measures. The 2008 crisis revealed a number of vulnerabilities in the economy, putting significant downward pressure on growth and prosperity. Since then, the government has responded with a number of important measures to stimulate job creation and productivity. Yet Slovenia still faces labour market challenges, related to the low participation rate of older workers, and the prevalence of skills shortages and mismatches in certain occupations.

The OECD Local Economic and Employment Development (LEED) Programme has developed its reviews on Local Job Creation as an international cross-comparative study that examines the contributions of local labour market policy to boosting quality employment and productivity. To help Slovenia respond to current and future labour market challenges, the review has looked at a range of institutions and bodies involved in employment and skills policies. In-depth case study work was undertaken in the Drava and South-East regions of Slovenia to understand implementation capacities and opportunities.

Overall, the review found that Slovenia has a dense network of organisations and actors working to increase job creation, innovation and competiveness. Slovenia is a small economy of 2 million people, but regions differ significantly in terms of local economic structure and consequently by unemployment and growth opportunities. The differences are even more pronounced at the municipal level. Despite its small size, Slovenia is divided into 212 municipalities. Often, the smallest or newly established municipalities are also those with the poorest infrastructure and lowest implementation capacities, which can cause a vicious cycle of unemployment and poverty. There are clear tensions between centrally-driven policies and those developed at the local level, which are sometimes targeted to a small number of companies or individuals. The following key conclusions and recommendations are intended to help build and expand on the recent and ongoing reforms to better promote inclusive job creation at the local level in Slovenia.

Key conclusions and recommendations

Better aligning programmes and policies to local economic development

- **Inject flexibility into the management of employment programmes and policies at the local level.** In particular, local employment services offices could be provided with a flexible budget envelope to design programmes and strategies for job creation in partnership with other actors, such as regional economic development organisations. This would ensure that programmes are more responsive to local labour market conditions.

- **Create a co-ordinated action plan for jobs and simplify institutional arrangements and responsibilities across the range of government organisations.** More should be done to co-ordinate policy planning for employment, skills and economic development at the national level. In addition, a board structure could be piloted across selected regions in Slovenia to bring together employment services, vocational education, economic development organisations with local employers. Such boards could be tasked with co-ordinating the relevant policy portfolios and provided with a funding envelope to introduce joint programmes under a regional employment and economic development strategy, linked with a national action plan for jobs.

- **Use local labour market information and intelligence to conduct more evaluations on the strengths and weaknesses of EU-funded projects.** The government should examine how to strengthen the evaluation of EU-funded projects to ensure that programmes with demonstrated success continue to be delivered and get prioritised over those which do not achieve the same results.

Adding value through skills

- **Create a well-functioning apprenticeship system that better connects training opportunities to the workplace.** While a new working group is planned to develop further advice in this area, there is a general lack of awareness about the future directions of apprenticeship in Slovenia. There is an opportunity for local stakeholders to play a critical role in fostering stronger business-education partnerships, which better connect training opportunities to workplace needs. The government should introduce programmes to foster these types of partnerships in order to promote participation in apprenticeship in strategic sectors of the economy.

- **Encourage participation in adult education by developing upskilling and retraining opportunities.** Life-long learning systems could be improved in order to provide workers – particularly those with low skills levels – with more opportunities for upskilling and retraining throughout their careers. Measures that could be considered include creating greater financial incentives for older workers to participate in higher education and training programmes, and paying closer attention to the design of such programmes so as to take into account the specific constraints of jobseekers and individuals that are currently in employment.

- **Strengthen local employer ownership of the design and delivery of skills development opportunities.** More opportunities need to be provided to local employers to participate in training programmes and advise Vocational Education and Training (VET) providers on their future skills needs. This can be achieved through formal collaboration within "spaces" or networks that give employers opportunities to advise training providers and other local partners, and through informal partnerships. Local leadership is crucial to reach out to employers and facilitate partnership working.

Targeting policy to local employment sectors and investing in quality jobs

- **Focus efforts on the better utilisation of skills to stimulate innovation and productivity.** The focused attention on developing competitive sectors within the Smart Specialisation Strategy of Slovenia, together with the inclusion of Human Resources Development and new approaches of inclusive multilevel governance (SRIPs), is welcomed. Going forward, the government should look for further opportunities to work with local employers to move them into higher value added production and re-organise work and jobs to make better use of talent in the workplace. Public procurement policies, financing mechanisms and local anchor institutions can play an important role in assisting employers to adopt high-performance workplace practices and create incremental innovation within a local economy.

- **Foster a stronger culture of entrepreneurship within the employment services, with a focus on the core working age population.** While a number of programmes and strategies are in place, more focus should be placed on programming to the general core working age population (as opposed to programmes only focused on youth).

Being inclusive

- **Continue to leverage the social enterprise sector to support inclusive growth.** The government should leverage opportunities within the social enterprise sector to support disadvantaged groups in reaching their full labour market potential.

Reader's guide

The *Local Job Creation* project involves a series of country reviews in Australia, Belgium (Flanders), Canada (Ontario and Quebec), Czech Republic, France, Ireland, Israel, Italy (Autonomous Province of Trento), Korea, Poland, Sweden, Turkey, the United Kingdom and the United States (California and Michigan). The key stages of each review are summarised in Box 1.

> **Box 1. Summary of the OECD LEED Local Job Creation Project Methodology**
>
> - Analyse available data to understand the key labour market challenges facing the country in the context of the economic recovery and apply an OECD LEED diagnostic tool which seeks to assess the balance between the supply and demand for skills at the local level.
> - Map the current policy framework for local job creation in the country.
> - Apply the local job creation dashboard, developed by the OECD LEED Programme (Froy et al., 2010) to measure the relative strengths and weaknesses of local employment and training agencies to contribute to job creation.
> - Distribute an electronic questionnaire to local employment offices to gather information on how they work with other stakeholders to support local job creation policies.
> - Conduct an OECD study visit, where local and national roundtables with a diverse range of stakeholders are held to discuss the results and refine the findings and recommendations.
> - Contribute to policy development in the reviewed country by proposing policy options to overcome barriers, illustrated by selected good practice initiatives from other OECD countries.

While the economic crisis is the current focus of policy-makers, there is a need for both short-term and longer-term actions to ensure sustainable economic growth. In response to this issue, the OECD LEED Programme has developed a set of thematic areas on which local stakeholders and employment and training agencies can focus to build sustainable growth at the local level. These include:

1. **Better aligning policies and programmes to local economic development challenges and opportunities**;
2. **Adding value through skills**: Creating an adaptable skilled labour force and supporting employment progression and skills upgrading;
3. **Targeting policy to local employment sectors and investing in quality jobs**, including gearing education and training to emerging local growth sectors and responding to global trends, while working with employers on skills utilisation and productivity; and,
4. **Being inclusive** to ensure that all actual and potential members of the labour force can contribute to future economic growth.

Local Job Creation Dashboard

Chapter 3 of this report provides a summary of the results of the Local Job Creation dashboard, which is a policy implementation capacity assessment tool developed by the OECD. As part of this international comparative project, the OECD has drawn on its previous research to develop a set of best practice priorities across four thematic areas, which is used to assess local practice and implementation capacities (see Box 2 for a list of the thematic areas and sub-indicators). A value between 1 (low) to 5 (high) is assigned to each of the indicators corresponding to the relative strengths and weaknesses of local policy approaches based on best practices in other OECD countries. These indicators are established by looking at a range of quantitative and qualitative data at the local level. The dashboard enables national and local policy-makers to gain a stronger overview of the strengths and weaknesses of the current policy framework, whilst better prioritising future actions and resources.

Box 2. Local Job Creation Dashboard

1. **Better aligning policies and programmes to local economic development**
    1.1. Flexibility in the delivery of employment and vocational training policies.
    1.2. Capacities within employment and VET sectors.
    1.3. Policy co-ordination, policy integration and co-operation with other sectors.
    1.4. Evidence based policy making.
2. **Adding value through skills**
    2.1. Flexible training open to all in a broad range of sectors.
    2.2. Working with employers on training.
    2.3. Matching people to jobs and facilitating progression.
    2.4. Joined up approaches to skills.
3. **Targeting policy to local employment sectors and investing in quality jobs**
    3.1. Relevance of provision to important local employment sectors and global trends and challenges.
    3.2. Working with employers on skills utilisation and productivity.
    3.3. Promotion of skills for entrepreneurship.
    3.4. Promoting quality jobs through local economic development.
4. **Being inclusive**
    4.1. Employment and training programmes geared to local "at-risk" groups.
    4.2. Childcare and family friendly policies to support women's participation in employment.
    4.3. Tackling youth unemployment.
    4.4. Openness to immigration.

The approach for Slovenia

The focus of this study is on the range of policies targeting job creation through the implementation of employment, skills, and economic development programmes. The purpose of the study is to describe and evaluate the effectiveness of these policies, in relation to similar approaches across the OECD. The methodology of the study is given by an analytical framework developed by the OECD and applied across a range of countries.

In-depth work was undertaken into two local case studies (South-East Slovenia and Drava) to understand the implementation of these policies. Interviews were undertaken with stakeholders in each region through group discussions and individual interviews (both in person and through email and phone). Each group consisted of representatives of the employment service, skills and training organisations, regional development agencies, local governments and social partners. Additionally, a survey was circulated among public employment service offices and 37 responses were received and analysed.

The OECD conducted a study visit to Slovenia in November 2015 to gather feedback on the findings of the review as well as potential recommendations to improve the overall framework for quality job creation and productivity. Roundtable meetings and project visits were held in each case study area as well as with national stakeholders.

References

Froy, F., S. Giguère and E. Travkina (2010), *Local Job Creation: Project Methodology*, OECD Local Economic and Employment Development (LEED), OECD Publishing, Paris.

Chapter 1

Policy context for employment and skills in Slovenia

This chapter provides an overview of the general economic situation in Slovenia and the most recent macroeconomic developments as well as their impact on labour market trends. Slovenia was one of the most profoundly hit economies in the 2008 downturn primarily because of its high reliance on export demand as well an unsustainable model of debt-financed investment and consumption demand. In 2015, unemployment was roughly twice as high compared to 2008. As the crisis continued, labour market outcomes, including long-term and youth unemployment, deteriorated. The government implemented a number of measures to directly support "keeping jobs" as well as tackle unemployment-related problems via active and passive labour market measures.

Economic and labour market trends

Slovenia experienced a period of solid and stable growth between 2000 and 2008 facilitated by a skilled workforce and solid industrial base. However, the 2008 crisis had a profound impact on the country, as exemplified by a 7.8% decline in Gross Domestic Product (GDP) in 2009. The severity of the crisis was the result of vulnerable trade linkages as well as declining external demand, which led exports to fall to 57% of GDP in 2009. The crisis also had a pronounced impact on gross capital formation, which declined by 32.2% in 2009.

Recovery has been slow and difficult, as the government initially reacted hesitantly in dealing with the causes of the crisis (OECD, 2015a). From 2010-11, growth slowly regained traction, but the economy dampened again between 2012 and 2014 (SORS, 2015). The decline in 2012 coincided with a cut in wages in the public sector (Republic of Slovenia, 2012). While household consumption and investment saw positive growth in 2014, state consumption has steadily declined since 2011 (SORS, 2015). In 2015, exports of goods and services gained momentum, reaching 77.9% of GDP (Eurostat, 2016).

Previous OECD analysis of Slovenia highlighted the need to strengthen the banking and corporate sectors, address rising debt levels in view of the pressures that will be created from population ageing, and introduce structural reforms to improve the overall labour market situation and create better quality jobs (OECD, 2015a).

Figure 1.1. **Growth rates of key economic indicators (%), 2000-15**

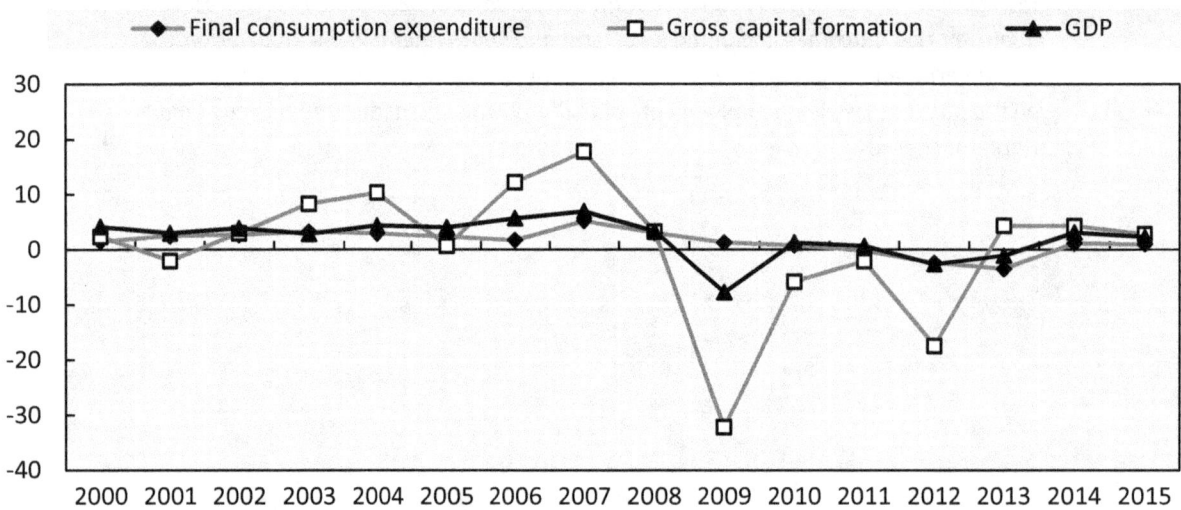

Source: OECD (2017a).

The global financial crisis impacted overall employment and affected the labour market position of many vulnerable groups, especially youth. This impact varied across sectors and regions in Slovenia (OECD, 2016e). The employment rate slightly declined from 68.6% to 65.2% between 2008 and 2015, and was higher for men (69.2% in 2015) than women (61%) (OECD, 2017b).

The unemployment rate went from 4.5% in 2008 to over 10% in 2013, which was above the OECD average. Two in three unemployed in Slovenia do not receive income support, which puts them at serious risk of poverty (OECD, 2016a). In all OECD counties, the level of qualification of individuals has an effect on the probability of being unemployed, but this effect is even greater effect in Slovenia (OECD, 2016a). In 2015, the unemployment rate for tertiary educated individuals was 5.8%, very close the EU average of 5.7%, but it reached 10% among upper secondary and post-secondary (non-tertiary) educated individuals and 17.8% among individuals with less than upper secondary education (Eurostat, 2016).

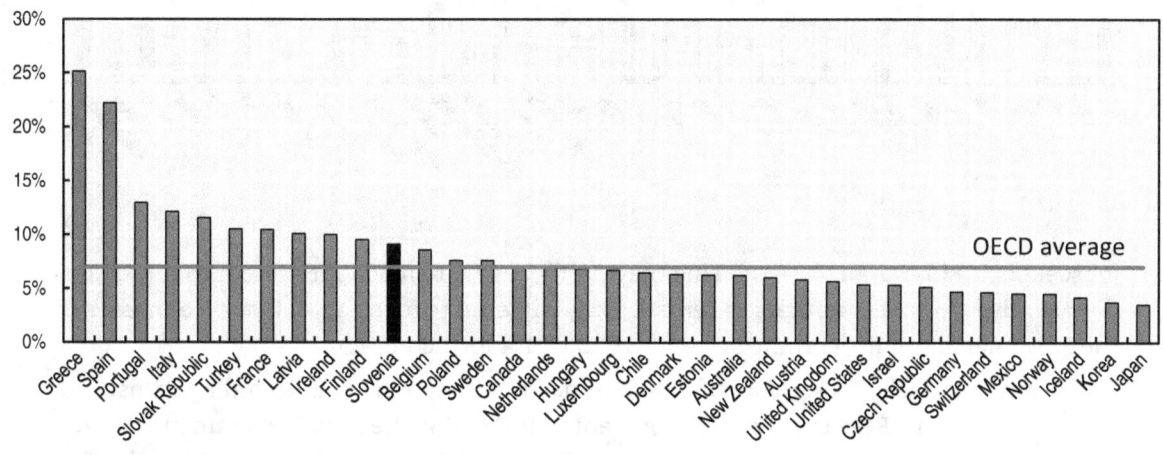

Figure 1.2. **Unemployment rate across OECD countries, aged 15-64, 2015**

Source: OECD (2017b).

The long-term unemployment rate also increased significantly following the crisis, reaching 5.3% in 2014 from a low of 1.9% in 2008 (Eurostat, 2016). While the long-term unemployed represented 42.2% of all unemployed in 2008, this proportion was 54.5% in 2014. The number of long-term unemployed that were unable to find work for 18-23 months is almost five times the number it was in 2008. Long-term unemployment has disproportionately impacted men. Between 2009 and 2012, the male share of total long-term unemployment reached 55% (Eurostat, 2016).

In the wake of the global financial crisis, the labour market outcomes for some particular groups have worsened considerably. For example, the employment rate of those workers with less than upper secondary education went from 56.2% in 2007 to 49% in 2015 (OECD, 2016a). This has led to a widening employment gap between individuals according to their level of educational attainment. Similarly, in 2014, unemployment was more than twice as high for low-skilled workers (15.4% compared to 6.1% for the high-skilled). While the active labour market policy system was effective in facilitating job-to-job transitions following the crisis, this system was not well adapted to helping unemployed persons with weak labour market attachment back into employment. Thus, the number of low-skilled unemployed and older workers has increased to constitute roughly half of total unemployed in 2015 (OECD, 2016a).

Youth were also severely impacted by the economic crisis in Slovenia, almost doubling the 15-24 year old unemployment rate to about 16.5% in 2015 (see Figure 1.3). Older workers are also facing severe difficulties in the labour market in view of the high levels of inactivity among this population (OECD, 2016a). The employment rate among the 55-64 year-olds stands at 35%, compared to 55% on average for this group in OECD countries. Slovenia also has the lowest retention rate among all OECD countries, which explains why one in three

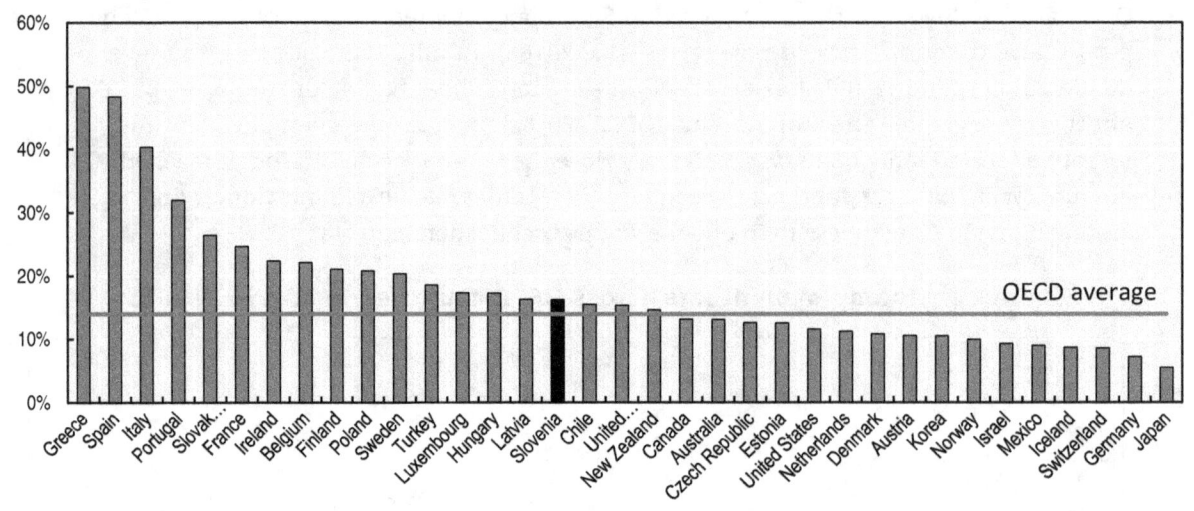

Figure 1.3. **Youth unemployment rate (15-24) across OECD countries, 2015**

Source: OECD (2017b).

jobseekers is older than 50 years. This may partly be due to a benefit system that provides disincentives for older workers to remain longer in employment as well as weaknesses in the Slovenian life-long learning system (OECD, 2017f forthcoming).

During the crisis, wages also suffered but the impact started later. According to Institute for Macroeconomic Research and Development (IMAD, 2013), the initial adjustments started in the private sector, primarily by cutting overtime, lowering working hours, and terminating temporary contracts. Wage growth was already slowing in 2009, but started to decline in late 2011 and stayed negative until 2014. Public sector wages also adjusted significantly, with nominal growth being halted following the 2012 "Law on balancing public finances", which nominally lowered wages by 8%. Another notable development was the public sector wage increase in 2008, which was a consequence of the changes in the public sector wage system (for further information on the reforms, see OECD, 2011).

Another one of the more discussed measures during the crisis was the minimum wage increase in 2010. The minimum gross wage in Slovenia is around EUR 790, while the average wage in May 2015 was EUR 1 528 (SORS, 2015). According to the latest Eurostat data (Eurostat, 2017), Slovenia has the highest ratio between the minimum and average wage in Europe; the minimum wage represents 51.3% of the average monthly wage in Slovenia. In comparison, the minimum wage represented 41% of the average monthly wage in 2008.

In recent years the wage distribution has been characterised by a "disappearing middle" effect (OECD, 2016a), which is a sign indicating that the job market in Slovenia is becoming increasingly polarised. Major job losses in medium-skilled occupations have been observed while the number of jobs requiring high levels of skills has grown steadily. This pattern of "job polarisation", which can be observed in other OECD countries such as Denmark and Estonia, is often the result of routine jobs being automated following the adoption of new technologies (Berger and Frey, 2016).

Education and skills

Educational attainment levels in Slovenia have improved significantly over the last decade (OECD, forthcoming, 2017e). The share of low educated people among the working age population (i.e. those who possess below upper secondary education) went from

20% in 2005 to only 13% in 2015, which is much lower than the OECD average of 23% (Figure 1.4). Although tertiary attainment was ten percentage points higher in 2015 (30%) compared to 2005 (20%), this remains below the OECD average of 35%. This is essential, as the level of qualification and skills have a large impact on individuals' labour market outcomes.

Figure 1.4. **Share of the population by educational attainment, aged 25-64, 2015**

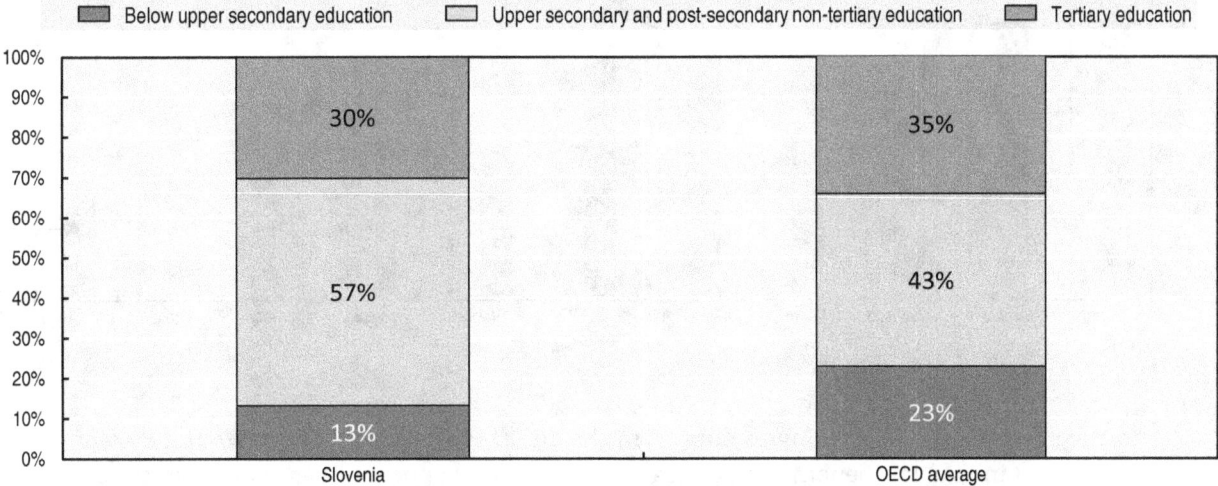

Source: OECD (2017c).

Low educational attainment of specific student-population groups (particularly Roma students) has been highlighted has a pressing challenge in Slovenia (OECD, 2016c). Individuals in the Roma community are less likely to be enrolled in pre-school education and they tend to leave education earlier, often after basic education.

According to the Survey of Adult Skills (PIAAC),[1] adults in Slovenia show below-average proficiency in both literacy and numeracy compared to adults in the other OECD countries (Figure 1.5), and around one in four adults performs poorly in these skills. In terms of problem-solving in technology-rich environments, only 3.7% of adults in Slovenia attain the highest proficiency level (level 3) while only 21.6% are proficient at level 2, compared to 5.8% and 25.7% respectively on average in OECD countries (OECD, 2016d). This lack of problem-solving skills is even apparent among the tertiary educated population, which is a major issue to attract potential investors (OECD, 2017f forthcoming).

Over the past two decades, literacy scores have improved significantly in Slovenia. However, this general improvement has not benefited the whole population equally, and considerable differences can be observed depending on socio-demographic characteristics such as age, socio-economic status, level of education and immigrant background (OECD, 2016d). In particular, native-born Slovenians and native-language immigrants tend to have much higher levels of literacy and numeracy than foreign-language immigrants. On average, younger generations are more proficient than older age groups in all three domains, which indicates that the level of skills within the Slovenian population should continue to improve in the future. But it should be noted that the generational gap is greater in Slovenia than in most other OECD countries. No significant differences between male and female outcomes can be observed in terms of skills proficiency levels in Slovenia.

Those individuals with low levels of skills may become trapped in a situation where they are not able to obtain the skills needed to access quality employment opportunities (OECD,

Figure 1.5. **Mean literacy and numeracy scores, OECD Survey of Adult Skills (PIAAC), selected OECD countries and OECD average**

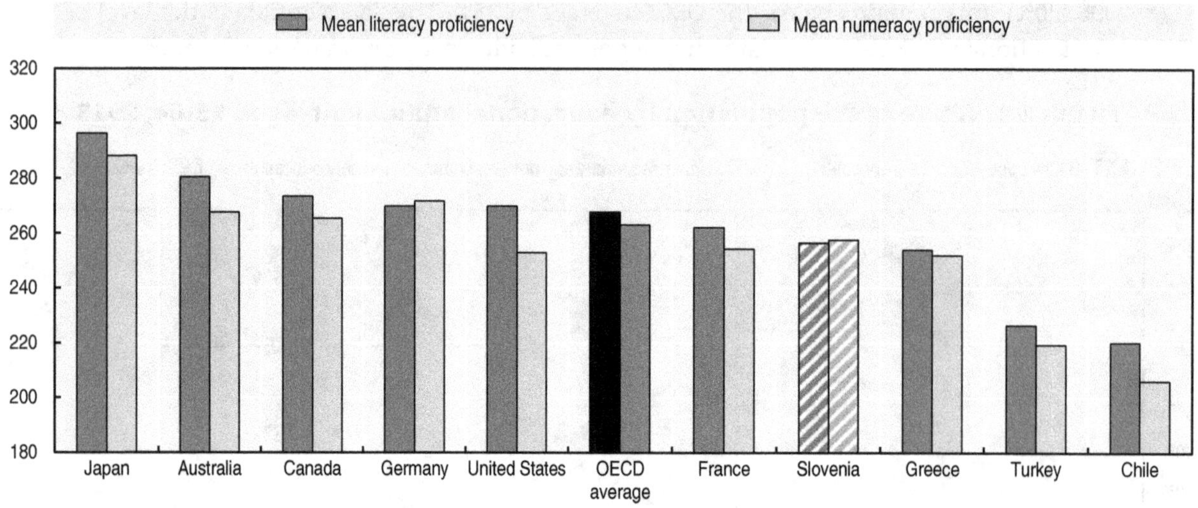

Source: Survey of Adult Skills (PIAAC) (2012, 2015).

forthcoming, 2017f). According to data from the OECD PIAAC survey, only around 30% of low-skilled individuals benefit from education and training opportunities, compared to 78% of adults with high levels of skills (OECD, 2016d). This large gap can be a serious obstacle to making the labour market more inclusive as labour force participation and employment prospects in Slovenia are much better for individuals with higher proficiency in literacy and numeracy, and information-processing skills have a strong positive impact on wages (OECD, 2016d). Similarly, the difficulties faced by older workers in remaining in the labour market may partly be explained by the low share of such workers seeking to participate in education or training programmes (OECD, 2016a). More generally, the relatively low share of individuals of all ages that engage in upskilling activities shows that more could be done to encourage life-long learning in Slovenia.

While most workers in Slovenia are well-matched with their jobs (OECD, 2016d), there is some indication that the education and training system is not fully able to provide skills that are demanded on the labour market. In particular, labour market mismatches for highly educated workers have tended to increase in recent years (OECD, 2016a). There are also signs of labour shortages in a number of vocational occupations, including mechanical engineering, computer science, construction, chemical technologies, and services such as catering and hotel management (ESS, 2017).

In recent years, the policy response to address such skills shortages has clearly prioritised offering better training opportunities to young people. But at the same time, life-long learning for those in employment has tended to be neglected (OECD, 2017f forthcoming). These gaps in the education and training system can have serious undesirable consequences for individuals, firms and society as a whole. Individuals may acquire skills that they will not be able to put to use in their job and firms may not be incentivised to move up the value chain if they are not able to secure the skilled workforce they need to operate their investment.

National policy context: Increasing competitiveness and growth

Several national strategies form the basis for the national government's labour market policy goals. These include the *Strategy for Economic Development of Slovenia 2006-13*, which sets a number of goals around increasing competitiveness and growth; boosting investments in research and development; improving institutional competitiveness and the overall functioning of the state; creating a modern welfare system and labour market; and promoting sustainable development. A new development strategy for Slovenia is also in preparation. It will include a strategic vision for 2050 as well as strategic planning priorities and measurable targets within the UN 2030 Agenda for Sustainable Development.

The *European EU2020 Strategy* includes targets such as boosting the employment rate to 75%; increasing R&D expenditure to 3% of GDP; reducing greenhouse gas emissions; boosting educational attainment such that 40% of 30-34 year-olds complete tertiary education; and ensuring a reduction of 40 000 in the number of people at risk of poverty or exclusion.

Additionally, *the Partnership Agreement between Slovenia and the European Commission for the period between 2014-20* provides policy and programme guidelines around a number of policy goals that have been set through the *Strategy for Economic Development of Slovenia 2006-13* and the *European EU2020 Strategy*. Finally, *the Operational Programme for the Implementation of the EU Cohesion Policy in the Period 2014-20* operationalises the partnership agreement and provides further details about the measures to support the achievement of the goals from the agreement.

In this context, the most important and recent strategy adopted by the government and approved by the European Commission in autumn 2015 is the *Smart Specialisation Strategy of Slovenia*. This strategy aims to 1) boost Slovenian competitiveness by increasing its innovation potential, 2) diversify the existing industrial structure (both in the manufacturing and services sector) and 3) promote the development and growth of SMEs. The strategy plays a key role in integrating development priorities outlined through the *Slovenia's Development Strategy 2006-13*, the Slovenian industrial policy and the Digital Agenda.

Slovenia is currently implementing a new phase of its *Smart Specialisation Strategy*, also called "S4". In order to achieve the strategic objective of S4 – developing sustainable technologies and services for a healthy life – and reach the targets set in terms of raising the value added per employee, a number of key principles are being pursued during the implementation of the strategy. These include integrating strategies in various policy domains, ensuring the consistency of the policy mix, and clearly defining strategic objectives and priorities. Tailored governance structures, including the newly created Strategic Research and Innovation Partnerships (SRIPs), have also being established with the aim of encouraging collaboration and co-operation of stakeholders. Specific measures are being rolled out as part of the S4 policy mix in the following areas:

- Increasing R&D and innovation by promoting basic and applied research, promoting co-operation and research in value chains, supporting investment, internationalisation, foreign direct investment (FDI), and better use of research infrastructure;
- Developing human resources by increasing research, promoting international mobility, strengthening development and innovation competencies, strengthening the knowledge and competences of employees and focusing on youth;
- Promoting entrepreneurship and innovation by focusing on start-ups, SMEs, and promoting knowledge transfer;
- Creating a supportive and development-oriented state.

These documents and strategies outline the basic goal of Slovenia's future development, which clearly show that Slovenia aims to move further into the most developed group of OECD countries and climb the value-added ladder.

Regional development strategies have also been promoted through a *Law on the promotion of Balanced Regional Development* that was passed in 2011 and subsequently amended in 2012. The objectives of this law were to curb interregional disparities, revive areas distressed by industrial shocks, achieve balanced growth and implement a new industrial policy building on innovation and smart specialisation (OECD, 2016f).

Employment policies and programmes

The main body for labour market policies in Slovenia is the Ministry of Labour, Family, Social Affairs and Equal Opportunities. It oversees and manages policies related to labour relations, activation, equal opportunities, and cohesion policies. Employers also play an active role through a number of business organisations, including the Association of Employers of Slovenia, the Chamber of Craft and Small Business of Slovenia and the Slovenian Chamber of Commerce. Among the associations of unions, the largest is the Association of Free Trade Unions of Slovenia and the Confederation of Unions of the Public Sector of Slovenia.

As clearly highlighted, the labour market has changed significantly since the beginning of the crisis. This has led the government to introduce a number of reforms and measures that aim to improve the overall efficiency and functioning of the labour market. One of these areas has been pension reform. The focus has been primarily on the pension/wage ratio and the extension of work for older workers, which was necessary because of an ageing workforce and increasing dependency ratios. Amongst EU countries, Slovenia is projected to have the third-highest rate in the costs of managing ageing (pensions, long-term care, health care, education, unemployment benefits) as a percentage of GDP, following only Greece and Luxemburg. The costs of managing ageing are expected to rise from around 23% to 36% of GDP between 2007 and 2060 (European Commission, 2009).

In response, the government introduced the Law on Pension and Disability Insurance (1999), which included gradual increases in the retirement age. The Law also strengthened the link between pensions and income (actual contributions) by extending the reference period for calculating pensions from 10 to 18 years. The Law has been supplemented and changed several times, including reforms to pension levels and retirement conditions in 2012. These changes were less rigorous than a previous proposed reform, which was introduced in 2011 but was never implemented or passed in Parliament because of strong union opposition.

Before the global financial crisis, efforts were being made in Slovenia to increase labour market flexibility. In 2007, the Law on Labour Market Relations was amended to allow better internal flexibility by facilitating employment for a specific job, extending the legal grounds for flexible employment, improving legislation about job contract termination and severance pay, increasing the flexibility of work arrangements, cutting down notice periods for layoffs, allowing additional overtime, and introducing more stringent discrimination clauses. A subsequent reform of the law was made in 2013 to further simplify job termination procedures, adjust the costs of terminating a work contract for an indefinite period, while also increasing the cost of fixed-term contracts.

In 2010, the Law on Labour Market Regulation was adopted, with the goal of further increasing labour market flexibility, lowering the impact of the unemployment trap, and reducing administrative barriers for employers. In 2010 the government had also made an ambitious plan to tackle the problem of undeclared work as well as to make the labour market more flexible through two laws: the Mini Jobs Law or the Law on the Prevention and

Detection of Undeclared Work and Employment, which covers "personal supplementary work". However, due to strong opposition from students and unions the Mini Jobs Law was rejected on a referendum in 2011.

> ### Box 1.1. Mini jobs and "personal supplementary work" for greater flexibility and security, 2010/14
>
> The concept of "personal supplementary work" was introduced as part of the Law on the Prevention and Detection of Undeclared Work and Employment. The introduction of "personal supplementary work" was an attempt to reduce the incentives for participation in the informal economy and provide benefits to workers in these types of occupations. Jobs that would typically qualify as "personal supplementary work" include domestic help, babysitting, producing and selling hand-made products and smaller and limited tasks for individuals or companies. Such jobs were typically done as part of the informal economy. Under the reforms, an individual must register as a provider and report income to the tax administration every half year in order to carry out supplementary jobs. In lieu of standard taxation, each provider would purchase a monthly coupon at the price of nine euros; Seven euros of which is used for pension insurance, and two contribute to health insurance. The total annual income of a provider of "personal supplementary work" should not exceed three average monthly net wages (roughly EUR 3 000 per year).
>
> The Law on Mini Jobs (which was rejected at a referendum in 2011) was intended to introduce "small or mini jobs" as paid, temporary or more permanent jobs for students and retired people. These jobs were limited in time to 60 hours per month (720 a year, with some additional flexibility for students). Yearly income was not to exceed EUR 6 000, while a minimum gross hourly wage was set to EUR 4 (93% of students earned less and would benefit). The income would be taxed by 14%. The collected revenues would be used by the state to pay primarily for scholarships, student facilities, student organisations, projects for students and retired, and active labour market policies. The Law was intended to allow retired people to improve their social position. Students would also benefit from small jobs by allowing them to obtain formally acknowledged work experience (which would facilitate future employment) while contributing to their pension. Unions and student organisations strongly opposed the law, arguing that it would further deteriorate the position of the young, increase the share of precarious jobs, lower employment opportunities of the young and impact their ability to obtain financing for studying.
>
> Nonetheless, as part of the 2013 Law on Labour Market Relations and within the 2014 Public Finances Stabilization Act, the government addressed the problems of work for students and the retired. Retired people are entitled to work up to 60 hours per month and are allowed to earn up to 6300 euros per year (and not less than 4.20 euros per hours) with temporary or occasional jobs. To avoid exploitation, employers are limited in the number of hours which can be dedicated to such types of jobs. Student work was still geared towards temporary tasks to allow for greater flexibility in both the demand and supply of labour. Nonetheless, by adding the social and health contributions to the cost of student work, the students gained rights (pension insurance and other rights) as well as work that was acknowledged as part of formal work experience. Moreover, since youth unemployment as well as the precariousness of jobs they are often forced to take have been recognized as a problem, the increased cost of student work also served to make "normal" employment of youth more attractive to employers. This also addresses the issues of young people studying several years longer than expected in order to retain student status to get work more easily.
>
> *Source:* Republic of Slovenia Ministry of Labour, Family, Social affairs and equal opportunities (2017).

During the recent crisis, the government also introduced other measures to support quality and sustainable employment conditions. More recently, the state has supported mentorship opportunities for youth as well as the implementation of the Youth Guarantee programme. The Youth Guarantee plan was adopted in 2014 in order to reduce the average unemployment spell among youth. During the crisis, youth were significantly affected by low labour market demand and job creation. In 2012, the government has set a target to reduce average unemployment amongst youth (15 to 29 years) from 10.65 months to 9.5 months by 2016. The Plan foresees that all young people registered with the public employment service would receive an offer of employment, training or further education within 4 months of registration.

The government prepared an extensive set of measures to tackle youth unemployment that could be broadly categorised into two groups. The first are preventive measures, which target youth while they are still in school. These include incorporating career guidance in regional career centres and universities, providing a system for documentation of non-formal learning, facilitating and promoting more work-based training (apprenticeships, and internships), promoting creativity, entrepreneurship and innovativeness in schools and universities, strengthening the programme of project learning and providing an extensive and targeted system of scholarships. As part of the S4 strategy, measures are being taken to address gaps that have been identified in terms of promoting entrepreneurial skills and supporting innovative projects by young people.

The second group encompasses activities which have been introduced to promote labour market integration. These include reforms to student work, strengthening the support and counselling services to youth, focusing more on enabling international mobility (EURES), and promoting entrepreneurship and innovation. Specific measures include the "Entrepreneurially Into the World of Business" programme, a new initiative to stimulate entrepreneurship and self-employment and promote university incubators and start-up programmes. The initiative also establishes different training and mentorship schemes, strengthens the National Vocational Qualifications system, develops special training and mentorship programmes and promotes employment by providing tax exemptions for employers introducing special regional schemes, and promoting university incubators, as well as different training and job-opportunities (including self-employment). In 2014, the plan was estimated to cost EUR 43 million, which was increased to EUR 50 million in 2015.

Employment Services

The key institution for implementing labour market policies is the Employment Service of Slovenia (ESS). The ESS is divided into 12 regional offices with associated local labour offices. The ESS is run by the general manager and the ESS council. The ESS council consists of 13 members, including representatives from the Government of the Republic of Slovenia, (employers, unions and the ESS). The central office and the leadership are responsible for planning the implementation of employment services and providing support for IT, analytics, legal, HR, financial, and accounting (ESS, 2015b).

The 12 regional offices are responsible for the implementation of tasks related to monitoring labour market trends at the local level, and supporting local offices in their co-operation with employers and ESS sub-contractors. The local offices are the direct link between the ESS and the clients and implement the policies of ESS (e.g. employment counselling, providing insurance for unemployment, and implementing employment policies) (ESS, 2015c). Figure 1.6 shows the distribution of ESS organisations and how they align with administrative NUTS 3 regions (Nomenclature of Territorial Units for Statistics), which are often used for statistical gathering and labour market information. As shown in the figure, the areas covered by regional ESS offices often cross multiple statistical regions in Slovenia.

Figure 1.6. **Geographical organisations of the Employment Services of Slovenia (ESS) and NUTS3 statistical regions**

ESS regional offices, left panel; NUTS3 regions, right panel

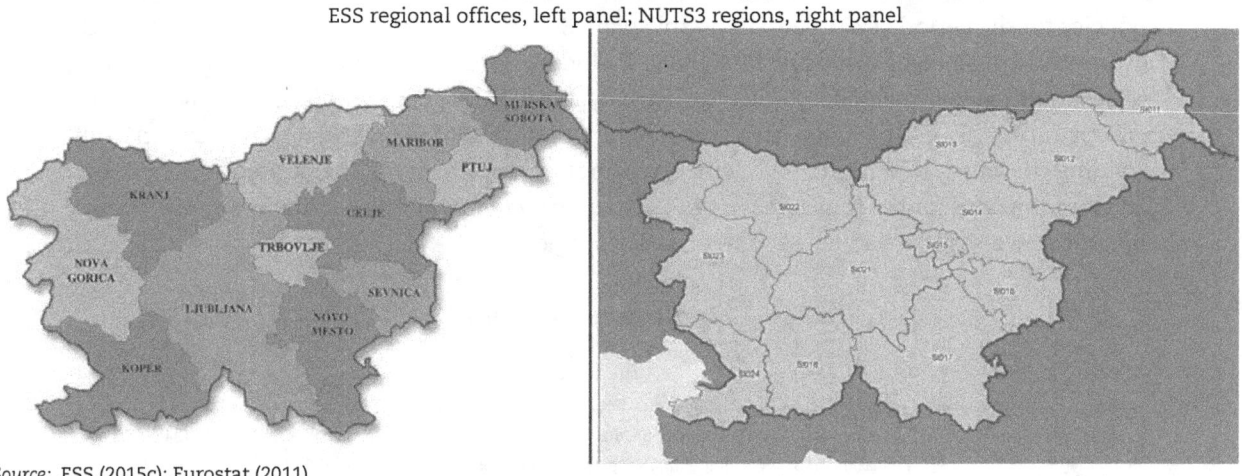

Source: ESS (2015c); Eurostat (2011)

Labour market policy measures can be broadly divided into active and passive labour market policy and employment protection legislation. In the past decade, Slovenia has been moving towards increased utilisation of active labour market policies, but the use of passive measures has also increased due to the crisis. In 2013, active labour market measures accounted for 0.37% of GDP while passive measures accounted for 0.8% of GDP. The funding for both measures is below the OECD average, which is 0.56% and 0.91% of GDP respectively.

Figure 1.7. **Public expenditure on active and passive labour market measures (LMP) as a percentage of GDP, 2014**

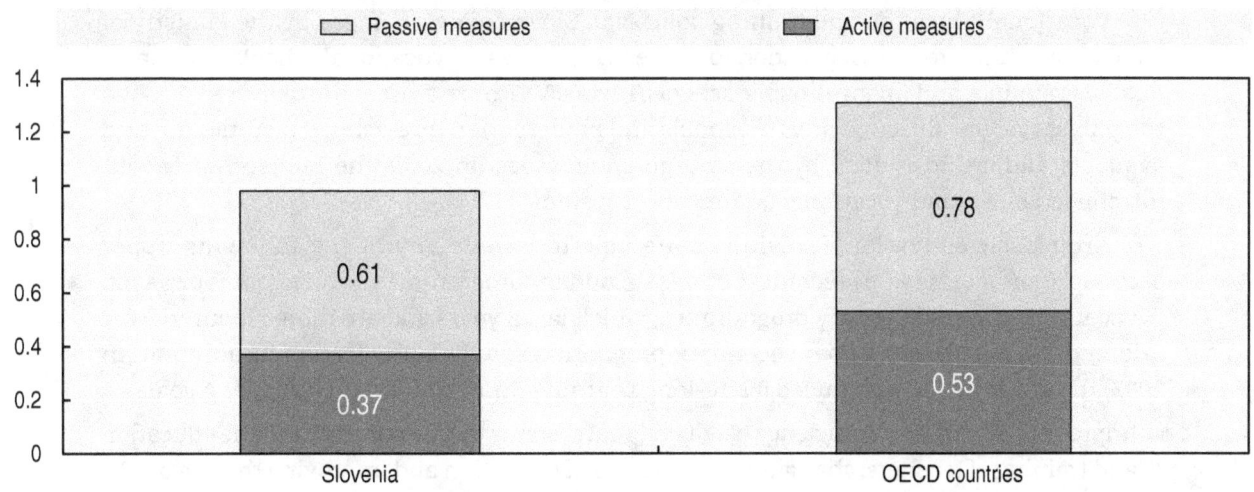

Source: OECD (2017b).

Slovenia spends less on labour market policy than other EU countries. In 2011, the EU28 spent 1.9% of GDP on average on labour market policy, while Slovenia only spent a total of 1.2% of GDP. In Slovenia, the amount spent on passive measures (supports) exceeds spending on active labour market policies by a factor of 3.5, while the average ratio for EU countries is 2.5. The total amount spent on labour market policies increased significantly since the beginning of the crisis, from 0.45% of GDP in 2008 to 1.2% in 2014.

Active labour market policies plan for 2016-20

In November 2015, the government introduced guidelines for active labour market policies for the period of 2016-20. Under this plan, EUR 100 million (roughly 0.25% of GDP) will be spent to achieve clearly specified goals, including: decreasing the number of the long-term unemployed; increasing both the employability and employment of disadvantaged groups (primarily young, older and low-skilled workers); and strengthening education and training measures in order to deal with structural unemployment. The strategy specifically stresses the need for the measures to be able to quickly respond to the situation in the labour market as well as to be adjusted to the needs of regions.

Table 1.1. **Indicators for Main Goals**

Goal	Indicator	Value in 2014	Target value for 2020
Lowering the burden of long-term unemployment	Lowering the number of long-term unemployed	59 859	40 000
	Increasing the share of long-term unemployed among those that get employment	24.9	33
Faster activation	Faster employment for those up to 29 years (average unemployment duration, months)	10.5	7
	Faster employment for those aged 50 and more (average unemployment duration, months)	34.5	30
Lowering structural imbalances	Lowering structural unemployment by increasing the number of those included in education and training	30 059	30 100
	Increasing the share of unemployed that have been employed within 6 months of completing education/training (%)	44.6	50

Source: Republic of Slovenia Ministry of Labour, Family, Social affairs and equal opportunities (2015).

Vocational education and training policies

Vocational education and training policies in Slovenia are managed by the Ministry of Education, which prepares legislation for upper secondary and vocational schools, maintains quality assurance and finances public schools. Formal VET programmes are delivered through the public system, although private schools and kindergarten (pre-school) facilities are also available and are co-funded by the state in some cases. In 2000, the Ministry of Labour introduced a national vocational qualification system.

After basic education, individuals are able to pursue any of the following upper secondary programmes: 1) technical upper secondary programmes, which last four years; 2) vocational upper secondary programmes, which last 3 years and are more labour market oriented; and 3) shorter upper secondary programmes, which are 2 years in duration. In 2007, the government introduced a Life-long Learning Strategy with the following goals:

- Improve the quality and efficiency of educational systems by investing in both the education and training of teachers, changing the structure of education and improving the use of ICT, in order to develop foundations for a knowledge society;

- Enable easier access to education and training to all and create an open educational environment, make education more appealing and link the educational goals to sustainable development goals (equal opportunities, social inclusion);
- Opening and linking the educational system into the broader context of the domestic and global economy by facilitating better linkages to the labour market and promoting international co-operation and exchange.

Adult education programmes are overseen by the Slovenian Institute for Adult Education (SIAE), the main national institution for research and development, quality and education, guidance and validation, and promotional and informative activities in the field of adult education. SIAE drafts professional bases and evaluations, and monitors the development of the adult education system, develops various non-formal and formal forms of learning, develops programmes to improve adult literacy, and pays particular attention to improving access by vulnerable groups of adults to education and learning. In doing so, it develops the necessary infrastructure to support learning, develops models for the self-evaluation of quality and the validation of prior learning, and provides professional education and training for adult educators. It carries out a number of tasks related to adult education, including the development of the system, preparation of programmes and teaching materials/methods, quality assurance, providing guidance and information about adult education programmes, conducting adult literacy research and training, and supporting the development and validation of non-formal learning activities. Their activities are also co-financed by the EU.

Vocational education and training is carried out through the national curriculum both for young and adults, but curriculum implementation is different for adults. The Institute of the Republic of Slovenia for Vocational Education and Training is responsible for the vocational education and training. Its tasks include overseeing the curriculum implementation in schools with regard to national vocational qualifications and occupational qualifications.

The qualification or certificate can be used either in the job search process or when enrolling in other educational programmes. Slovenia also offers a network of 14 "consulting centres", which carry out activities on behalf of the Slovenian Institute for Adult Education (ISIO, 2015) to support individuals in finding and completing the appropriate educational programmes. In addition, there are 32 self-study centres, which offer counselling and mentoring services and feature spaces for informal education. The participants can learn IT, languages and the use of internet. Overall, Slovenia has a well-developed VET system which provides various educational pathways for the development of skills.

Economic development and regional governance

Slovenia is divided into two cohesion regions (NUTS2) and 12 NUTS3 regions. The cohesion regions are Zahodna (Western) and Vzhodna (Eastern Slovenia). Western Slovenia comprises four NUTS3 regions (Central Slovenia, Upper Carniola, Gorizia, Coastal-Karst), while the rest are part of Eastern Slovenia. In general terms, Western Slovenia is more developed than the Eastern Slovenia.

Regional economic development strategies are prepared at several different institutional levels. The head organisation is the Ministry of Economic Development and Technology, which co-ordinates several bodies that work on different aspects of economic development and regional policy. The Ministry co-ordinates 12 regional development agencies as well as the public fund for regional and rural development. They support the preparation of legislation and regional development programmes (Ministry of Economic Development and Technology, Regional Development, 2015). In terms of cohesion policy, the Government Office for Development and European Cohesion Policy is the main institutional actor and acts as the Managing Authority for the European Structural and Cohesion Fund in Slovenia.

Figure 1.8. **Slovenian regions**

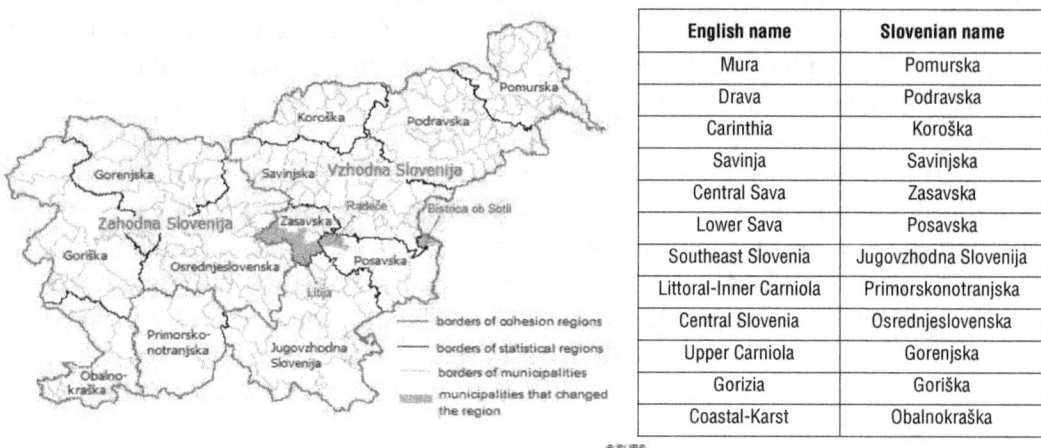

English name	Slovenian name
Mura	Pomurska
Drava	Podravska
Carinthia	Koroška
Savinja	Savinjska
Central Sava	Zasavska
Lower Sava	Posavska
Southeast Slovenia	Jugovzhodna Slovenija
Littoral-Inner Carniola	Primorskonotranjska
Central Slovenia	Osrednjeslovenska
Upper Carniola	Gorenjska
Gorizia	Goriška
Coastal-Karst	Obalnokraška

Source: SORS (2015).

Slovenia had the fourth lowest regional disparities in GDP per capita in OECD countries in 2010 (OECD, 2015a). Among Slovenian regions, Central Slovenia contributes most to Slovenian GDP (37.3% in 2013). The Drava region is second (12.9%), followed by Savinja (11.4%). Southeast Slovenia contributes 6.6% to GDP (SORS, 2015). Central Slovenia is the most developed region; its GDP per capita is almost 42% above the Slovenian average. Costal-Karst region is the second most developed, followed by South-East Slovenia with 95% of Slovenian average GDP per capita in 2013. Generally, the Mura, Lower Sava and Drava regions have the highest unemployment rates. The crisis increased the unemployment rates across Slovenia, but the increase between 2008 and 2013 was most pronounced in the Central Sava region and Coastal Karst, where the difference was above 8.6 percentage points.

The differences in economic development are also reflected in wages. Figure 1.10 presents an index of wages for May 2015, when gross average wage for Slovenia was EUR 1 528. Central Slovenia with the capital city of Ljubljana has wages that are 12% above the Slovenian average, while all other regions are below the Slovenian average. Other structural characteristics (gender differences, age differences) characteristics of the labour market also vary across regions. The specific industrial structure of some regions or proximity to the border (which results in more people working abroad) means these aspects become more or less pronounced.

Figure 1.9. **Unemployment rate by region, 2008 and 2015**

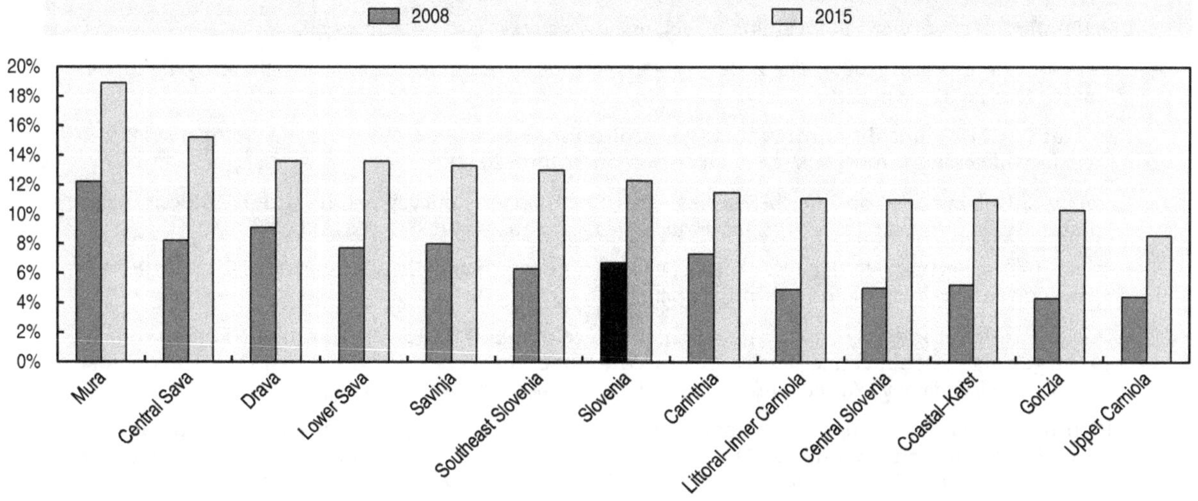

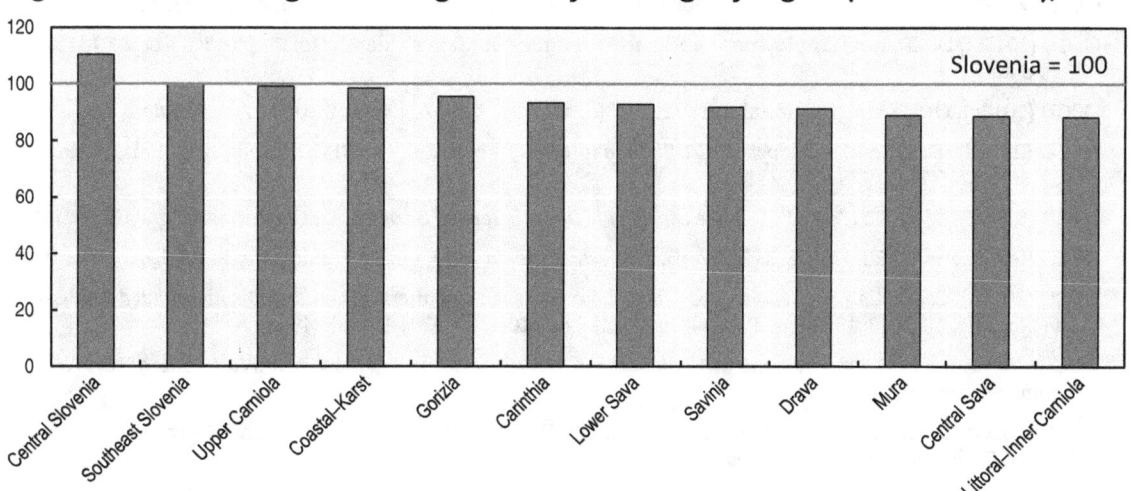

Source: SORS (2017).

Figure 1.10. **Index of gross average monthly earnings by region (Slovenia = 100), 2015**

Source: SORS (2017).

Note

1. The Survey of Adult Skills is a product of the OECD Programme for the International Assessment of Adult Competencies (PIAAC). It assesses the proficiency of adults aged 16 or more in literacy, numeracy and problem solving in technology-rich environments. In Slovenia, 5 331 adults aged 16-65 were surveyed between 1 April 2014 and 31 December 2014.

References

Berger, T. and C. Frey (2016), "Structural Transformation in the OECD: Digitalisation, Deindustrialisation and the Future of Work", *OECD Social, Employment and Migration Working Papers*, No. 193, OECD Publishing, Paris, http://dx.doi.org/10.1787/5jlr068802f7-en.

ESS (Employment service of Slovenia) (2017), Napovednik Zaposlovanja 2016/II [Employment Forecast 2016/II], www.ess.gov.si/_files/9382/NAP-ZAP_2016_II.pdf.

ESS (Employment service of Slovenia) (2015a), About ESS, http://english.ess.gov.si/about_ess.

ESS (Employment service of Slovenia) (2015b), ESS organization, http://english.ess.gov.si/about_ess/ess_organization..

ESS (Employment service of Slovenia) (2015c), www.ess.gov.si/_files/28/zrsz_os.gif.

European Commission (2009), *The 2009 Ageing report*, http://ec.europa.eu/economy_finance/publications/publication13782_en.pdf 18.

Eurostat (2017), "Monthly minimum wages – bi-annual data", http://ec.europa.eu/eurostat/en/web/products-datasets/-/EARN_MW_CUR, (accessed on 27 June 2017).

Eurostat (2016), Eurostat on-line "LFS series – detailed quarterly survey results (from 1998 onwards)", database, http://ec.europa.eu/eurostat/en/web/products-datasets/-/LFSQ_URGAED.

Eurostat (2011), *Regions in the European Union, Nomenclature of territorial units for statistics NUTS 2010/EU-27*, Eurostat methodologies and Working Papers, ISSN 1977-0375.

IMAD (Institute for macroeconomic research and development) (2013), Spremembe stanja in reforme na trgu dela v obdobju krize [The changes in the labour market during the crisis], IMAD, Ekonomski izzivi, www.umar.gov.si/fileadmin/user_upload/publikacije/izzivi/2013/trgdela.pdf.

ISIO (Informativno svetvalna dejavnost v izobraževanju odraslih [Information and consulting in support of adult education]) (2015), Mreža svetovalnih središč za izobraževanje odraslih [Network of Adult Learning Centers], http://isio.acs.si/sredisca/.

Ministry of economic development and technology (2015), Regional development, www.mgrt.gov.si/en/areas_of_work/regional_development/regional_development/.

OECD (2017a), OECD.Stat "National accounts at a glance" (database), http://dx.doi.org/10.1787/na-data-en.

OECD (2017b), OECD.Stat "Employment and Labour Market Statistics" (database), http://dx.doi.org/ 10.1787/lfs-data-en.

OECD (2017c), OECD.Stat "Regional Innovation" (database), http://dx.doi.org/10.1787/region-data-en.

OECD (2017d), *OECD Skills Outlook 2017: Skills and Global Value Chains*, OECD Publishing, Paris, http://dx.doi.org/10.1787/9789264273351-en.

OECD (forthcoming, 2017e), *OECD Skills Strategy diagnostic report: Slovenia*, OECD Publishing, Paris.

OECD (forthcoming, 2017f), *OECD Economic Surveys: Slovenia 2017*, OECD Publishing, Paris.

OECD (2016a), *Connecting People with Jobs: The Labour Market, Activation Policies and Disadvantaged Workers in Slovenia*, OECD Publishing, Paris, http://dx.doi.org/10.1787/9789264265349-en.

OECD (2016b), *OECD Employment Outlook 2016*, OECD Publishing, Paris, http://dx.doi.org/10.1787/empl_outlook-2016-en.

OECD (2016c), *Education policy outlook: Slovenia*, OECD Publishing, Paris, www.oecd.org/slovenia/Education-Policy-Outlook-Country-Profile-Slovenia.pdf.

OECD (2016d), Slovenia – Country Note – *Skills Matter: Further Results from the Survey of Adult Skills*, OECD Publishing, Paris.

OECD (2016e), *Job Creation and Local Economic Development 2016*, OECD Publishing, Paris, http://dx.doi.org/10.1787/9789264261976-en.

OECD (2016f), *OECD Regional Outlook 2016: Productive Regions for Inclusive Societies*, OECD Publishing, Paris, http://dx.doi.org/10.1787/9789264260245-en.

OECD (2015a), *OECD Economic Surveys: Slovenia 2015*, OECD Publishing, Paris, http://dx.doi.org/10.1787/eco_surveys-svn-2015-en.

OECD (2015b), *OECD Employment Outlook 2015*, OECD Publishing, Paris, http://dx.doi.org/10.1787/empl_outlook-2015-en.

OECD (2014), *Job Creation and Local Economic Development*, OECD Publishing, Paris, http://dx.doi.org/10.1787/9789264215009-en.

OECD (2011), *OECD Public Governance Reviews, Interim Paper: Review of the Slovenian Public Sector Salary System*, London: OECD.

Republic of Slovenia Ministry of Labour, Family, Social affairs and equal opportunities (2017), "Študentsko delo bo še naprej pomemben institut na trgu dela (izhodišča za ureditev)", ["Student work will continue to be an important institute in the labor market"], www.mddsz.gov.si/nc/si/medijsko_sredisce/novica/article/1939/7308/, (accessed 23 June 2017).

Republic of Slovenia Ministry of Labour, Family, Social affairs and equal opportunities (2015), "Smernice za izvajanje ukrepov aktivne politike zaposlovanja za obdobje 2016–2020", ["Guidelines for the implementation of active employment policy measures for the period 2016-2020"], *www.mddsz.gov.si/ fileadmin/mddsz.gov.si/pageuploads/dokumenti__pdf/zaposlovanje/Smernice_APZ_2016_2020__final.pdf.*

Republic of Slovenia (2012), "Znižanje plač ob hkratni odpravi plačnih nesorazmerij", ["Reducing wages, while eliminating wage disparities"], *www.vlada.si/teme_in_projekti/arhiv_projektov/varcevanje/ javni_usluzbenci/.*

SORS (Statistical office of the Republic of Slovenia, 2017), SI-STAT "Data by Statistical Regions", (SORS on-line database), *http://pxweb.stat.si/pxweb/Database/Regions/Regions.asp.*

SORS (Statistical office of the Republic of Slovenia, 2015), Data on territorial units according to the new situation of municipalities and regions, *www.stat.si/StatWeb/en/News/Index/4927.*

Survey of Adult Skills (PIAAC) (2012, 2015), Table A2.1. (*http://dx.doi.org/10.1787/888933366458*), Table A2.4 (*http://dx.doi.org/10.1787/888933366458*).

Chapter 2

Overview of the Slovenian case study areas

In-depth field work has been undertaken for this study in the South-East Slovenia and Drava regions, both of which are located in Eastern Slovenia. This chapter provides details about the general economic development and employment outcomes in both regions which differ in terms of industrial structure as well as labour market challenges.

Overview of the Drava and South-East Slovenia regions

Previous OECD research has found evidence of significant differences between Slovenian regional labour market in terms of the level of skills of the workforce and the demand for skills by employers, as well as employment and job creation trends (OECD, 2014; OECD, 2016a). Banerjee and Jesenko (2015) also found significant regional variation in terms of GDP per capita in Slovenia, which can be explained for a large part by differences in labour productivity as well as employment rates (OECD, 2016b). However, when looking at the spatial distribution of income, the gap between Slovenian regions is relatively small compared to other OECD countries (OECD, 2016c), due in part to significant commuting flows between regions. Slovenia is also a fairly balanced country in terms of indicators of well-being such as access to basic services, education and health (OECD, 2016c). As part of this OECD study, in-depth analysis was undertaken to look at the labour market challenges and policy actions that have been taken in the regions of Drava and South-East Slovenia.

The Drava and South-East Slovenia regions in brief

Both regions are part of the Eastern cohesion region, which is less developed on average than the Western region of Slovenia. However, when looking at regional GDP per capita (Figure 2.1), one can see that South-East Slovenia compares favourably to other regions within Slovenia, while the Drava region falls in the middle range of performance.

Figure 2.1. **GDP per capita index, Slovenian regions (Slovenia = 100), 2015**

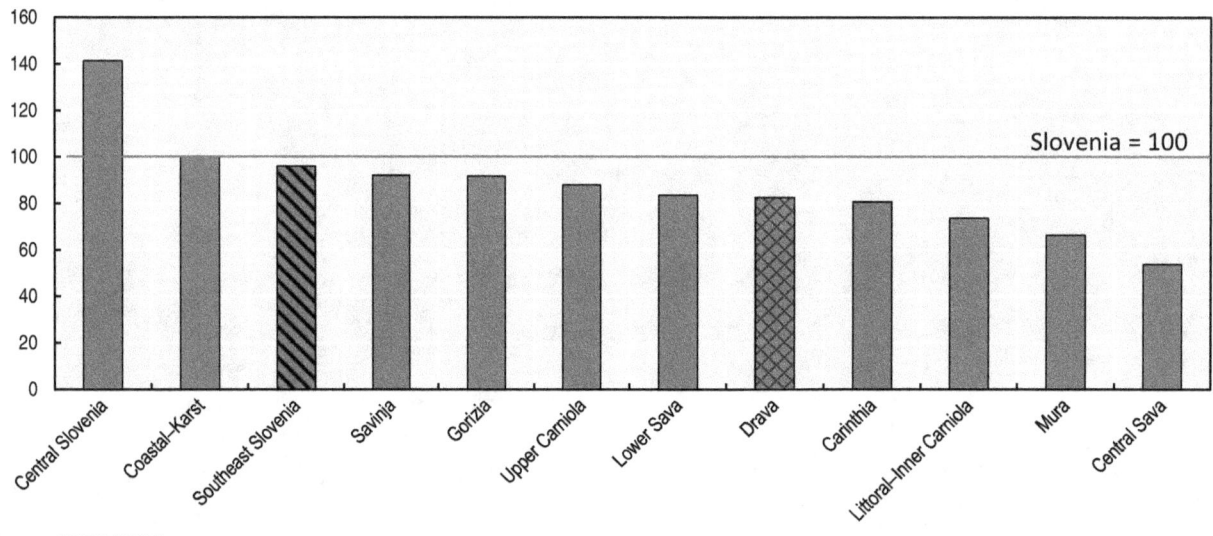

Source: SORS (2017).

South-East Slovenia is a highly diverse region, both geographically and economically. A large part of the region is covered by forest, and the hilly terrain has historically contributed to relatively poor transport connections within the region as well between the region and other parts of Slovenia. The two major cities of the region (Kočevje and Ribnica) gravitate more towards the region of Central Slovenia and the capital Ljubljana, while Bela Krajina (the region around the Kolpa river) gravitates towards Novo mesto, the capital of the South-East Slovenia region, which is also a strong industrial centre.

In South-East Slovenia, Osilnica and Kostel are the two smallest municipalities comprising 36 and 56 square kilometres and a population of 386 and 650 people respectively. These two municipalities are among the poorest in the region, and feature an ageing labour force with generally low skill levels. Novo mesto is the largest municipality with 236 square kilometres and a population of 36 000. In 2013, the average wage in Slovenia was EUR 997, while Osilnica had the lowest average wage in Slovenia at only EUR 693. On the other hand, Novo mesto municipality, which hosts two industrial giants in Slovenia (Krka, the pharmaceutical company, and Revoz, producing Renault cars) as well as several other strong companies (Adria Mobil, TPV) had an average net wage of EUR 1 116, significantly above the national average and the third highest among Slovenia's 212 municipalities. The region has several other industrial and economically strong municipalities. Ribnica municipalitiy is home to the Riko compny, an engineering firm with a number of high quality jobs. Trebnje was until recently known for Trimo, a construction sector company. Šmarješke and Dolenjske Toplice are known for thermal tourism, and several other locations are also pursuing niche tourism markets.

The Drava region is located towards the north-east of Slovenia, bordering Austria on the north and Croatia on the south. The largest municipality is the regional capital Maribor with 148 square kilometres and a population of 111 000. The municipality with the highest average net wage is Ruše with EUR 1 118, while Maribor (the regional capital) falls just below the Slovenian average of EUR 997 with an average of EUR 966. The poorest municipality in the region was Starše, which ranks just above Osilnica (South-East Slovenia) with EUR 702.

The region was hit hard by industrial decline, leading to significant unemployment, but efforts are being made promote local employment and economic development opportunities. Several large companies are located in the region, which has become more service-oriented. Among industrial firms, the metal industry remains important (Talum, Mariborska livarna), as well as the construction sector (Nigrad, Stavbar, AJM). Similarly, there are large employers in the agricultural and food processing (Perutnina Ptuj, Košaki, Jeruzalem) and in services (Terme Maribor, Terme Ptuj, Sintal, Varnost Maribor).

Regional economic development and the impact of the crisis

The Drava and the South-East Slovenia regions vary in terms of economic structure and development. For example, South-East Slovenia has quadrupled its GDP (in constant prices) since 1995. The Drava region increased its GDP by a factor of 3.6 over the same period. The global financial crisis had a significant impact on both regions. Between 2008 and 2014, aggregate output declined by annual average rate of 1.6% in the Drava region and 1.4% in the South-East Slovenia region.

The two regions differ significantly in terms of industrial structure. While the Drava region is relatively similar to the Slovenian average, South-East Slovenia has the highest share of manufacturing jobs in the country. It is also the most important exporting region, contributing the majority to Slovenia's exports of goods. During the past 15 years, the role of manufacturing in South-East Slovenia has increased from 39.7% of GDP in 2000 to 45.2% in 2013. A strong manufacturing sector gives the region significant growth and development

Figure 2.2. **Regional GDP annual average growth rate, 2001-07 and 2008-14**

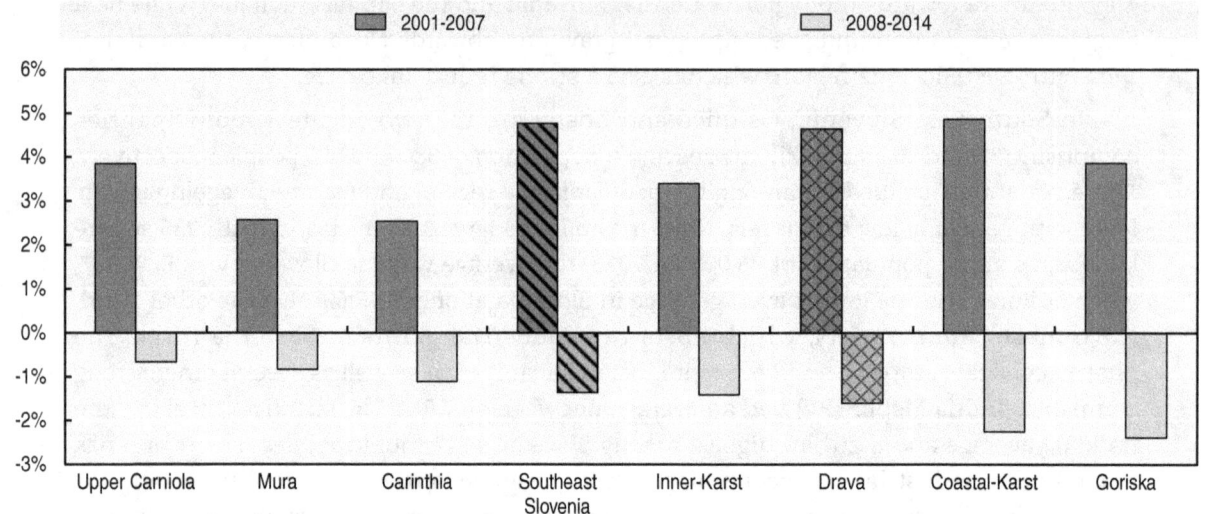

Source: SORS (2017).

potential due to value chains, trickle-down effects, knowledge and technology absorption (Greenwald and Stiglitz, 2014). In addition, the strong manufacturing core also provides a stable environment for the development of supporting services and the overall services sector. High wages attract talent and contribute to the development of intangible capital in the region.

The South-East Slovenia region has been expanding its ecological orientation in agriculture, where both vegetables and wine remain important products. Agriculture also facilitates employment to an increasing number of farmers; 17 co-operatives in the region support their work. Wood represents a major natural resource in the region, especially in Kočevska, where forests cover almost 80% of the area, well above the Slovenian average of 60% (SORS, 2015). Construction has remained relatively strong even during the crisis. On the other hand, the economic performance of the region varies between municipalities. For example, while Novo mesto and Trebnje are economically stronger, the deteriorating economic situation in Bela Krajina (Črnomelj, Metlika) and in Kočevska (Kočevje, partially Ribnica) is contributing to the loss of human capital. The remaining labour forc is often structurally unemployed with skills pertaining to traditional industries from the area (e.g. textile, wood, construction).

The Drava region has a strong industrial legacy from socialism, but the majority of big companies have been closed. While many medium and even larger companies have emerged and contribute to sustaining the industrial tradition, the potential for industrial development is strong. Maribor is a university centre with good infrastructure (e.g. an airport) and geographic and transport links to Austria and economic connections to former Yugoslav markets.

The region is also an energy centre due primarily to hydro-plants on the Drava River. It also has significant tourism potential (e.g. skiing and spa activities in Maribor, Pohorje, Ptuj). But in comparison to the South-East Slovenia region, the Drava region has a smaller number of larger industrial companies to drive broader development. Similar to the South-East Slovenia region, entrepreneurship is under-developed. In comparison with the South-East

Table 2.1. **Overview of the case study regions**

	South-East Slovenia	Drava
Economic activity	• Industrially strongest • Very export oriented • Technologically intense • High investment in R&D • Agriculture developing • Services not as developed, but tourism and trade important	• Industrially not strong, but strong industrial legacy (today only few larger companies) • Low value added, low productivity, low research and innovation intensity • Service sector underdeveloped
Main advantages/ opportunities	• Strong industry • Potential for value chain effects • Learning by exporting • Potential for development in wood industry and expansion of tourism • Higher education centre and research centre, also in co-operation with local economy	• University centre with strong human capital potential • Good infrastructure connections • Potential for industrial development as well as service development • Tourism development due to natural conditions as well as natural heritage • Strong local initiative and motivation to develop and support social entrepreneurship
Weaknesses	• Internal diversification and undeveloped parts of sub regions – Bela Krajina and Kočevska • Less developed entrepreneurship and SME sector • Structural unemployment • Human capital loss especially in sub-regions • High increase in unemployment during the crisis	• Low investment potential • Lack of entrepreneurial and business skills • Small number of new ventures • Structural unemployment

Slovenia region, the Drava region has low productivity and lower value added activities, as well as lower R&D activity. The region also lacks investment potential from domestic as well as foreign companies.

Labour markets in the South-East Slovenia and Drava regions

Labour market trends in both regions generally followed the patterns of economic activity at the national level over the past few years. Unemployment has increased between 2010 and 2013 in both regions, but less in the Drava region than in the South-East Slovenia region (Figure 2.3). Unemployment figures in the Drava region were significantly poorer than the national average at the peak of the crisis, but the region has seen major improvements in recent years, including for long term unemployment. The South-East Slovenia region has experienced a more severe deterioration of its labour market conditions. The regional unemployment rate increased by more than four percentage points between 2010 and 2013, and remained higher in 2016 (11.7%) compared to 2010 (10%). The long-term unemployment rate also increased sharply in the region and, at 7.2%, was much higher than the national average in 2016. The biggest changes in the unemployment rate in the South-East Slovenia region were in the less-developed municipalities of Črnomelj and Kočevje.

Looking at unemployment by age groups in both regions in comparison to the national average, one can see a U shape showing the highest levels of unemployment for youth between the ages of 15-24 year in both 2010 and 2014. Older age groups (e.g. 55-59) also have a higher unemployment rate than their younger cohorts. The unemployment rate of 25-29 year olds in the Drava region is also significantly above the national average.

Education levels have improved in all regions, with increasing shares of employed people with tertiary education and decreasing shares of low qualified workers. Both Drava and South-East Slovenia have levels of education slightly lower than the overall national average. In both regions, one can see significant growth in the number of individuals who possess tertiary education between 2005 and 2015. This trend aligns with the overall impressive growth in tertiary education levels in all regions of Slovenia (OECD, 2016c).

2. OVERVIEW OF THE SLOVENIAN CASE STUDY AREAS

Figure 2.3. **Registered unemployment in selected regions**

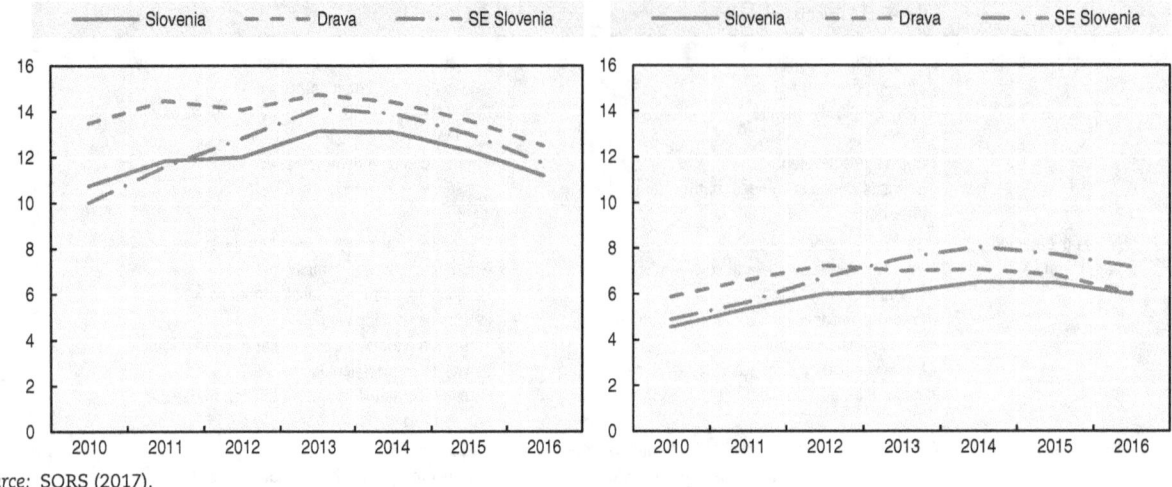

Source: SORS (2017).

Figure 2.4. **Unemployment rate by age groups, selected Slovenian regions, 2010 and 2015**

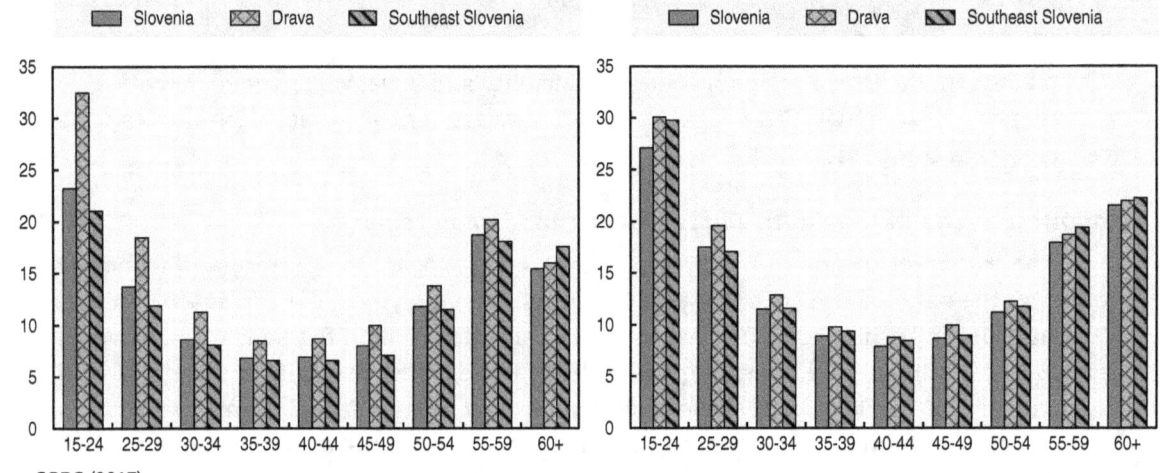

Source: SORS (2017).

Figure 2.5. **Educational structure of employed by region, 2005-15**

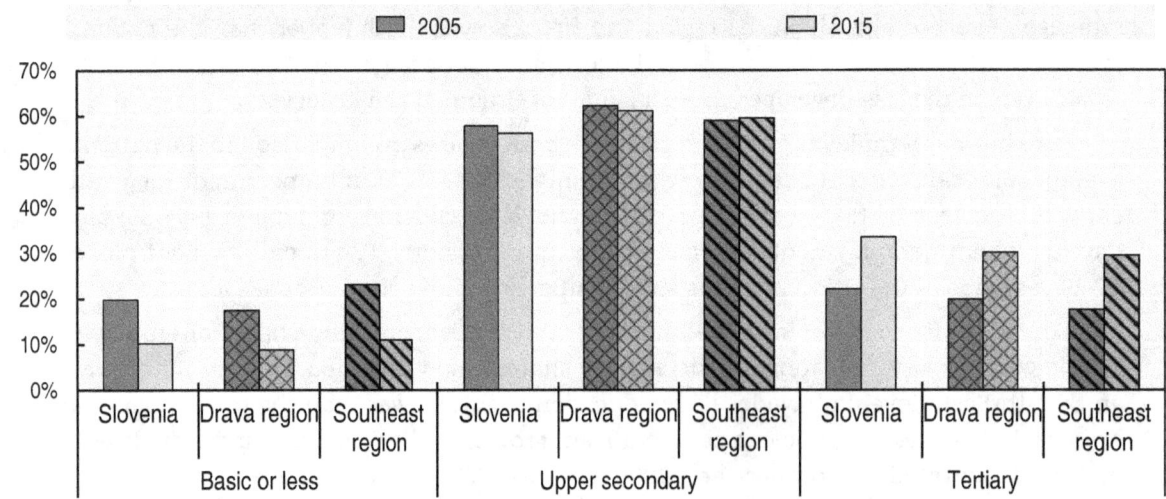

Source: SORS (2015).

Balance between skills supply and demand at the sub-national level

To supplement the above analysis within this chapter, the OECD LEED Programme has developed a statistical tool to understand the balance between skills supply and demand within local labour markets (Froy, Giguère and Meghnagi, 2012). In the Slovenian context, this tool can supplement the previous analysis to provide policy makers with an understanding of potential skills mismatches that may be occurring at the sub-national level. It can also inform place-based policy approaches at the local level on specific challenges and opportunities related to skills.

The analysis is carried out at Territorial Level 3 regions (regions with populations ranging between 150 000-800 000). The supply of skills was measured by the percentage of the population in employment with post-secondary education. The demand for skills was approximated using a composite index: percentage of the population in employment having medium to high skilled occupations and Gross Value Added (GVA) per worker (weighted at 0.25 and 0.75 respectively). The indices are standardised using the inter-decile method and are compared with the national median. Further explanations on the methodology can be found in Froy, Giguère and Meghnagi (2012).

Looking at Figure 2.6, in the top-left corner (skills gaps and shortages), demand for high skills is met by a supply of low skills, a situation that results in reported skills gaps and shortages. In the top-right corner, demand for high skills is met by an equal supply of high skills resulting in a high skill equilibrium. This is the most desired destination for all high performing local economies. At the bottom-left corner the demand for low skills is met by a supply of low skills resulting in a low skill trap. The challenge facing policymakers is to get the economy moving in a north-easterly direction towards the top-right corner. Lastly, in the bottom-right corner, demand for low skills is met by a supply of high skills resulting in an economy where what high skills are available are not utilised. This leads to

Figure 2.6. **Understanding the relationship between skills supply and demand**

Skills demand	Skills gaps and shortages	High skills equilibrium
	Low skills trap	Skills surplus

Skills supply

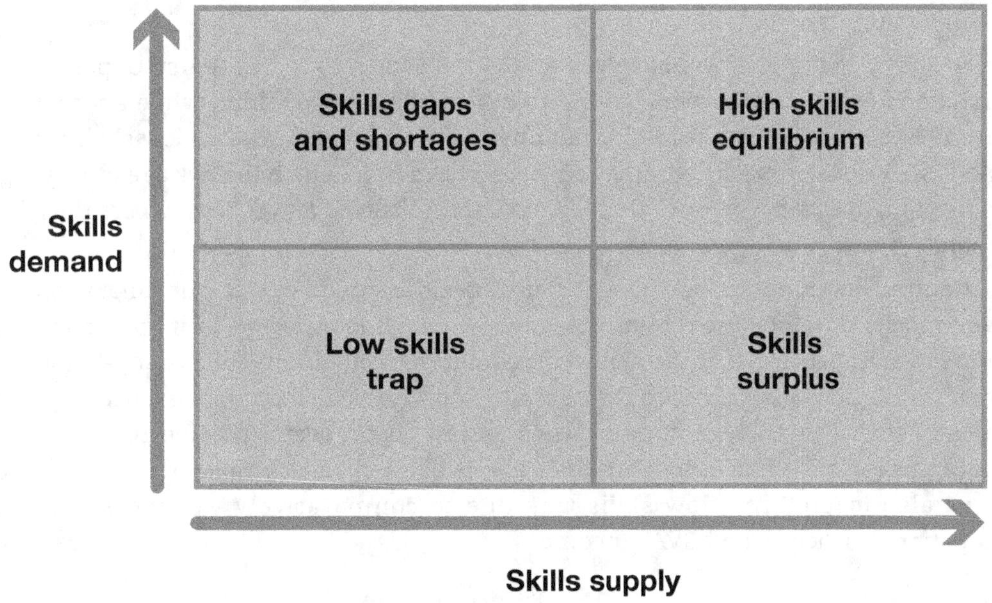

Source: Froy, F. and S. Giguère (2010), "Putting in Place Jobs that Last: A Guide to Rebuilding Quality Employment at Local Level", *OECD Local Economic and Employment Development (LEED) Working Papers*, No. 2010/13, OECD Publishing, http://dx.doi.org/10.1787/5km7jf7qtk9p-en.

the out migration of talent, underemployment, skill under-utilisation, and attrition of human capital, all of which signal missed opportunities for creating prosperity.

This typology is applied to regions in Slovenia in Figure 2.7 which shows how the country's 12 sub-regions (NUTS3) compare to each other in terms of skills supply and demand in the year 2013. As proxies for skills supply and demand, the tool considers educational attainment on the supply side (X-axis), and occupational structure and regional Gross Value Added figures on the demand side (Y-axis). Being in high skills equilibrium can be a good indication that a region is characterised by innovative and dynamic sectors.

Figure 2.7. **Balancing Skills Supply and Demand in Slovenia, 2013**

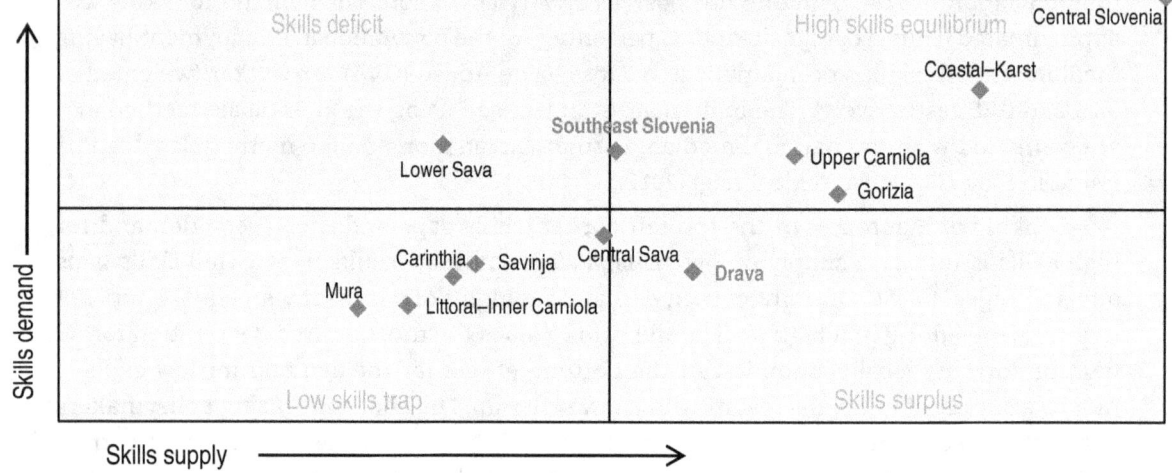

Source: SORS (2014a); SORS (2014b); SORS (2014c).

The results of the diagnostic exercise can also be seen through the country map of Slovenia (Figure 2.8), which clearly shows the divisions between the east and west of Slovenia in terms of skills mismatches.

In 2013, 5 of the 12 Slovenian regions – Central Slovenia, Coastal-Karst, Upper-Carniola, Gorizia and Southeast Slovenia – fell into a high skills equilibrium, while another five – Central Sava, Savinja, Carinthia, Littoral-Inner Carniola and Mura – in a low skills trap. Two regions showed an unbalanced situation in skills, Drava, in which there is a relatively higher supply of high-skilled workforce than demand for skills, and Lower Sava, where the relative demand for such a workforce exceeds the relative supply.

Central Slovenia Region, which encompasses the capital city of Ljubljana, is the most economically developed region in the country, which is reflected in its position on the graph in the upper corner of the high skills equilibrium quadrant. The Coastal-Karst region is the only region with access to the sea, which provides a comparative advantage in the tourism sector. The trade, accommodation and transport sector provide 36% of the total GVA of this region. While Inner Carniola had one of the highest employment rates in 2013, it was also located in a low skills trap due to comparatively weaker educational, occupational structure and GVA outcomes.

Figure 2.8. **Balance of Skills Supply and Demand in Slovenia, 2013**

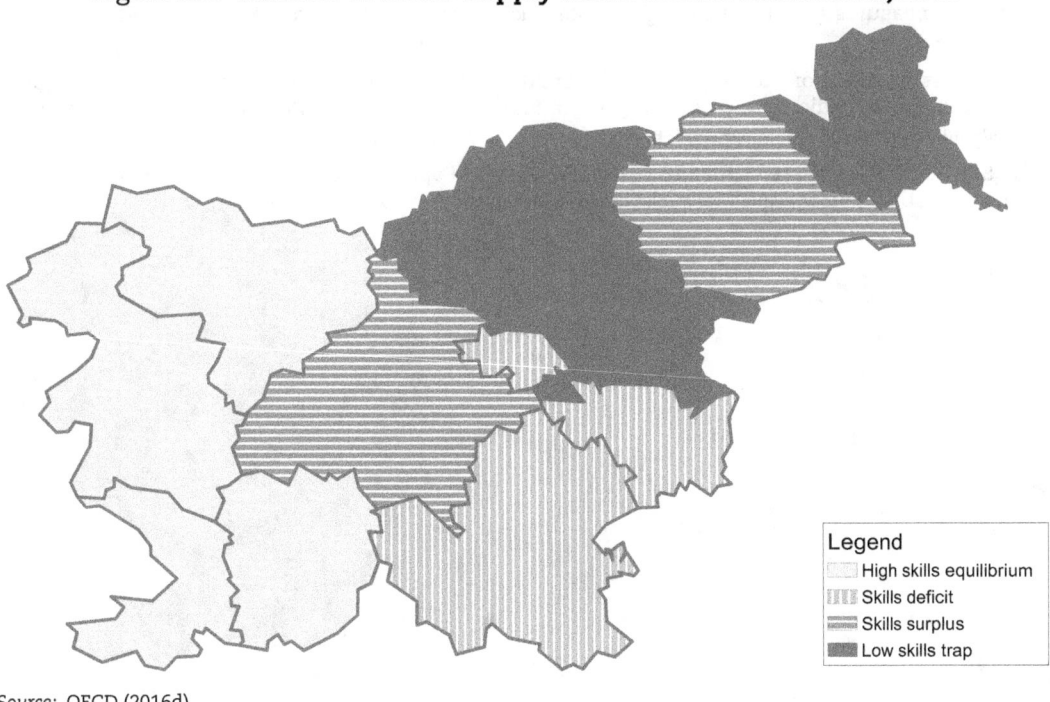

Source: OECD (2016d).

References

Banerjee, B. and M. Jesenko (2015), "Economic Growth and Regional Disparities in Slovenia", *Regional Studies*, Vol. 49/10, pp. 1722-1745.

Froy, F., S. Giguère, and M. Meghnagi (2012), "Skills for Competitiveness: A Synthesis Report", *OECD Local Economic and Employment Development (LEED) Working Papers*, No. 2012/09, OECD Publishing, http://dx.doi.org/10.1787/5k98xwskmvr6-en.

Froy, F. and S. Giguère (2010), "Putting in Place Jobs that Last: A Guide to Rebuilding Quality Employment at Local Level", *OECD Local Economic and Employment Development (LEED) Working Papers*, No. 2010/13, OECD Publishing, http://dx.doi.org/10.1787/5km7jf7qtk9p-en.

Greenwald, B.C. and J.E. Stiglitz (2014), *Creating a Learning Society: A New Approach to Growth, Development and Social Progress* (First Annual Lecture in Honnor of Kenneth Arrow at Columbia University) (New York: Columbia University Press).

OECD (2016a), *Job Creation and Local Economic Development 2016*, OECD Publishing, Paris, http://dx.doi.org/10.1787/9789264261976-en.

OECD (2016b), *Connecting People with Jobs: The Labour Market, Activation Policies and Disadvantaged Workers in Slovenia*, OECD Publishing, Paris, http://dx.doi.org/10.1787/9789264265349-en.

OECD (2016c), *OECD Regions at a Glance 2016*, OECD Publishing, Paris, http://dx.doi.org/10.1787/reg_glance-2016-en.

OECD (2016d), "Slovenia", in Job Creation and Local Economic Development 2016, OECD Publishing, Paris, http://dx.doi.org/10.1787/9789264261976-40-en.

OECD (2014), *Job Creation and Local Economic Development*, OECD Publishing, Paris, http://dx.doi.org/10.1787/9789264215009-en.

SORS (Statistical office of the Republic of Slovenia) (2017), SI-STAT "Data by Statistical Regions" (SORS on-line database), http://pxweb.stat.si/pxweb/Database/Regions/Regions.asp.

SORS (Statistical office of the Republic of Slovenia) (2015), "Med delovno aktivnimi osebami je bilo v letu 2014 več kot polovica medobčinskih delovnih migrantov", [Among persons in employment, in 2014, more than half were Intermunicipal working migrants], www.stat.si/StatWeb/prikazi-novico?id=5160&idp=3&headerbar=2.

SORS (Statistical office of the Republic of Slovenia) (2014a), "Regional Gross Value Added by year, NACE activity, measures and statistical region", *Statistical Office of the Republic of Slovenia, Regional Accounts* (database).

SORS (Statistical office of the Republic of Slovenia) (2014b), "Employed persons by statistical regions (NUTS3) and by major groups of occupation, Slovenia (in 1000)", *Statistical Office of the Republic of Slovenia, Regional Accounts* (database).

SORS (Statistical office of the Republic of Slovenia) (2014c), "Population by sex, age, statistical region, year and education", *Statistical Office of the Republic of Slovenia, Population* (database).

Chapter 3

Local Job Creation dashboard findings in Slovenia

This chapter presents the results from the OECD's local job creation dashboard, which was applied to Slovenia. The results are presented to compare how Drava and Southeast Slovenia are managing and implementing programmes along the following dimensions: 1) better aligning of policies and programmes to local employment development, 2) adding value through skills, 3) targeting policy to local employment sectors and investing in quality jobs, and 4) inclusion.

3. LOCAL JOB CREATION DASHBOARD FINDINGS IN SLOVENIA

Results from the dashboard

As part of this OECD Review on Local Job Creation policies, in-depth fieldwork and research was undertaken to assess local employment and economic development practices using a dashboard methodology developed by the OECD LEED Programme. The dashboard is divided into four thematic areas of analysis, which look at a range of policy and programme measures to understand implementation practices on the ground. A value of 1(low) to 5 (high) is assigned to each indicator based on the strengths and weakness of the policy approach, with a focus on its implementation in the two local case study areas. In this chapter, each of the four thematic areas of the study is presented and discussed sequentially, accompanied by an explanation of the results. The full results of the OECD Local Job Creation dashboard in Slovenia are presented in Figure 3.1 below.

Figure 3.1. **Local job creation dashboard results for Slovenia**

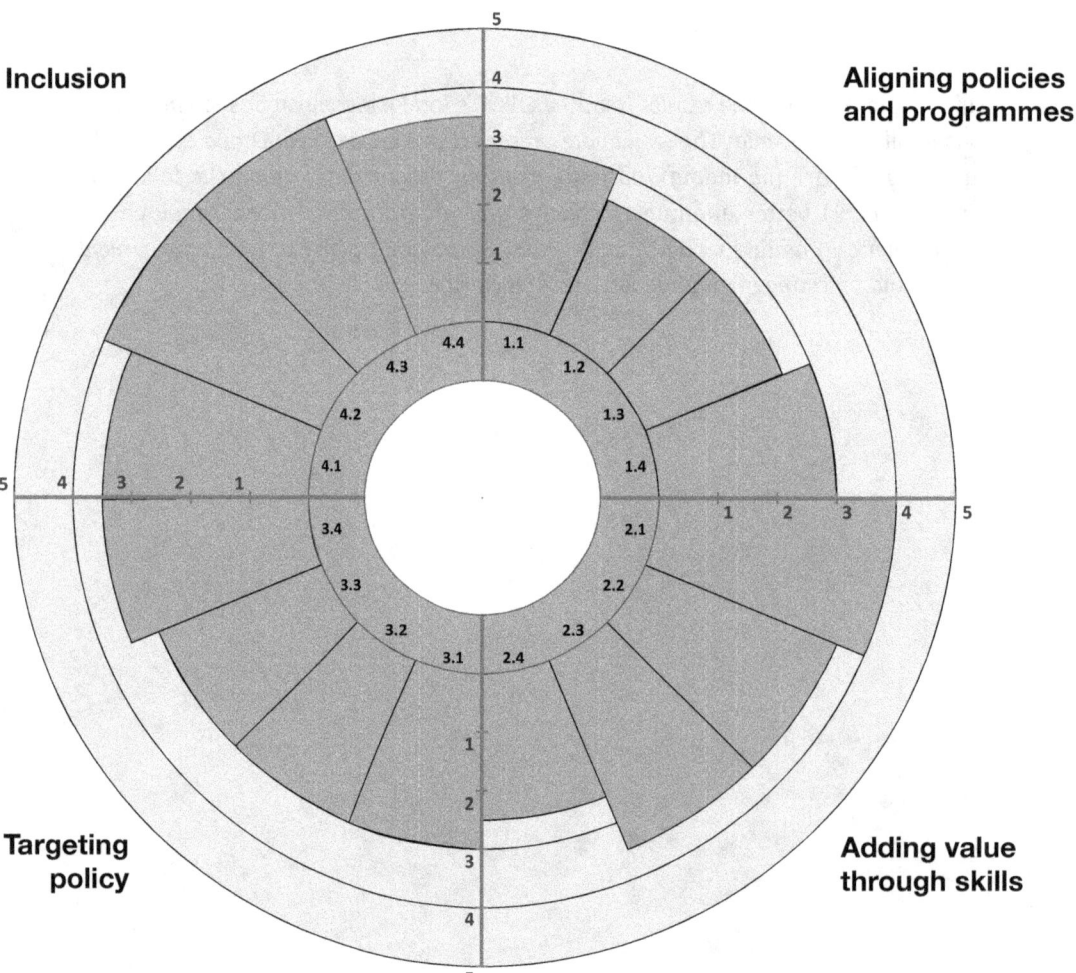

Theme 1: Better aligning policy and programmes to local economic development

Figure 3.2. **Dashboard results for better aligning policy and programmes to local economic development**

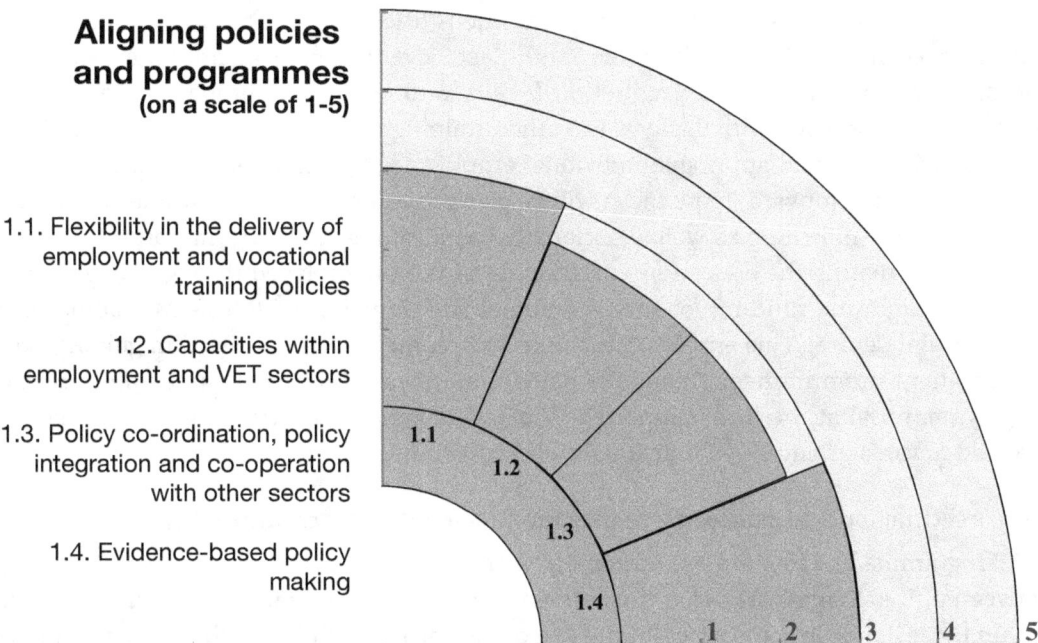

Flexibility in the delivery of employment and vocational training policies

The OECD defines flexibility as "the possibility to adjust policy at its various design, implementation and delivery stages to make it better adapted to local contexts, actions carried out by other organisations, strategies being pursued, and challenges and opportunities faced" (Froy et al., 2011). Flexibility deals with the latitude that exists in the management of the employment system, rather than the flexibility in the labour market itself. The achievement of local flexibility does not necessarily mean that governments need to politically decentralise (Froy et al., 2011). Governments just need to give sufficient latitude when allocating responsibilities in the fields of designing policies and programmes, managing budgets, setting performance targets, deciding on eligibility, and outsourcing services.

In Slovenia, labour market programmes and strategies are designed at the national level. Local and regional employment service offices can give advice about the perceived needs of the local economy during the preparatory stages of policy. However, most programmes provide limited flexibility to local public employment services (PES) offices to design their own strategies and initiatives to boost job creation. During the OECD study visit, it was highlighted that local and regional stakeholders would prefer to have more influence on the selection of measures to be implemented to ensure they are suited to local labour market conditions.

Local employment service offices are provided with operational flexibility through the development of individual employment plans. Under this mechanism, each unemployed individual is counselled and an employment plan is prepared based on the individual's skills, aspirations, and available job opportunities in order to find the best job match. This enables local PES offices to guide and facilitate individuals to specific programmes based on client suitability.

In addition, local PES offices have the ability to prepare specific training programmes in co-operation with local employers. Several such tailor-made programmes have been implemented. In Bela Krajina within the South-East Slovenia region, an important Slovenian company was opening a new production facility and needed a number of well-trained welders. In co-operation with the local PES office, training was organised for the unemployed with suitable skills and applicable individual employment plans to guide them into these jobs locally. Going forward, more focus will be given to tailor-made programmes in order to improve the job-matching as well as rationally use local resources. An important measure includes stimulating the education and training of the unemployed through active labour market programme funding for inter-company training centres (MIC – Medpodjetniški Izobraževalni Centre). This enables companies to become actively involved in guiding skills development programmes. This skills development programme includes a six month employment trial at the firm, supported by active labour market funding. The measure is targeted towards unemployed individuals who are often low skilled.

Target setting, budget and performance management and accountability

Programme budgets are set nationally with minor adjustments or transfers allowed between offices. Targets are set at the national level and the central office verifies spending within these limits. In some cases, at the end of the fiscal year, it is possible to move funding between programmes if funding is under-spent. However, a key issue is how budgets are assigned to regional and local offices. In some specific cases, quotas are not assigned to regional/local offices and spending is done on a "first come, first serve" basis, rather than on the prioritisation of resources and local needs.

Performance targets in Slovenia are set nationally for different policies and programmes. Targets include inputs (e.g. people enrolled into a programme), outputs (e.g. completion rates), as well as specific outcomes, such as lowering the unemployment rate. Targets are set based on statistical indicators and local offices are consulted on the preparation of these measures. In addition, the PES conducts surveys that measure the satisfaction of clients (e.g. the unemployed and employers) with their services. Once targets are set, the regional and local PES offices are accountable only to the central PES office and not to the local community.

Outsourcing

Outsourcing of activities is carried out nationally through a "registry" of potential providers. All potential providers must apply to be included in the "registry". Public calls are made for those organisations that would like to be included into the catalogue of those who can help in case of outsourcing activities. Local/regional PES offices can request the registration of a local provider. By registering, the provider becomes eligible to operate specific programmes.

In the past, a common criticism of employment services operations was that efficiency and costs were given priority over the quality of services and job placements. In response, the PES have reduced the evaluation criteria for selecting contractors based on the costs of services to 20%. Local PES offices have previously argued that they have limited influence over the choice of contractor and structure of contract. The lack of experience of some providers in delivering employment services in a local area has lessened the efficiency and effectiveness of some programmes, especially when contractors were not willing or able to make operational adjustments for a specific local target group (e.g. Roma, disabled).

Capacities within employment and VET sectors

As of 2013, Slovenia spends 0.37% of GDP on active measures, placing it in the bottom half of OECD countries in terms of relative spending (OECD, 2015a). The PES is financed through a combination of the integral state budget as well as European and national "projects". During the OECD study visit, local PES stakeholders acknowledged the importance of EU project-based financing to boosting the overall employment and skills budget. EU funding can often be used to finance programmes that are outside nationally set targets and may be more appropriate for specific groups (e.g. Roma programmes through the European Social Fund).

At the same time, however, there are also challenges associated with this type of EU based project funding, namely that it can be unpredictable or unsustainable. While core PES services and programmes are financed on a systematic basis, there are a number of staff and services at risk if certain EU project funding envelopes are discontinued. Some local PES offices report that up to 40% of overall programmes and services depend on EU-project financing. Even if programmes demonstrate good results, they can often be discontinued in the next project financing cycle or become temporarily unavailable once a given year's project budget has been spent out.

Figure 3.3 shows the results of an OECD questionnaire distributed to local PES offices. Financial resources and the number of staff are perceived as the most significant barriers to improving overall performance with the employment services. Local PES offices perceive the overall skills levels of staff and their level of local labour market knowledge as sufficient and not a barrier to the improvement of overall performance. Despite these results, it was noted during the OECD study visit that it would be beneficial to have more specialised personnel with background in psychology to work as front-line counsellors.

Figure 3.3. **Regional and local barriers to Public Employment Services (PES) performance improvements**

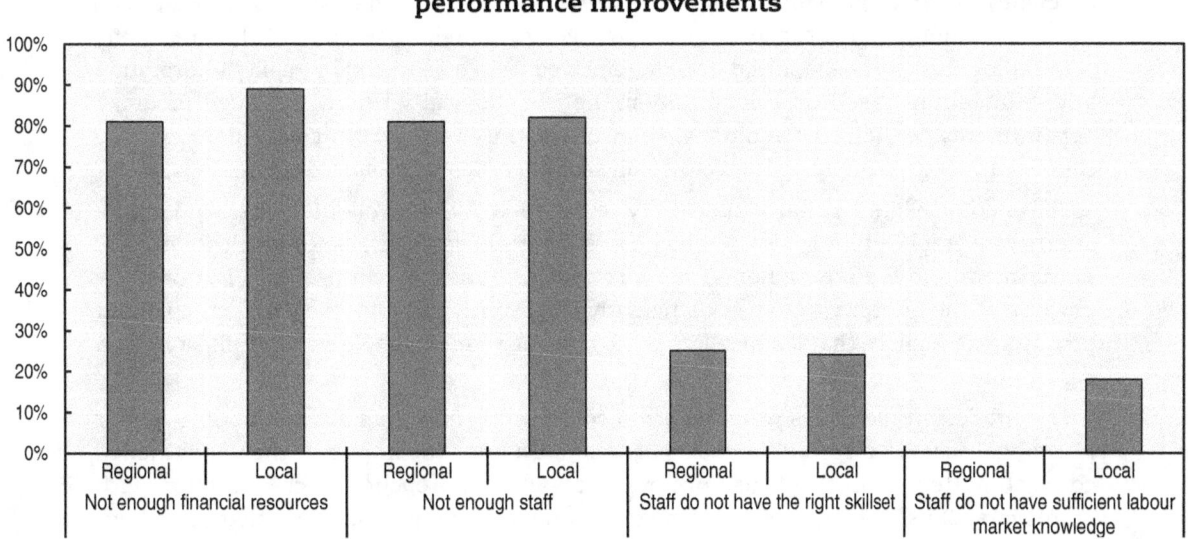

Source: OECD Public Employment Services Questionnaire.

During the OECD study visit, it was reported that some front-line staff are under pressure with the current level of unemployment and staff have had difficulty ensuring quality services and counselling in some cases. Hiring more caseworkers in order to reduce client-to-staff ratios may be necessary in order to increase the clients' chances of finding employment, and may pay for itself as the initial investment would be offset by lower benefit expenditure (OECD, 2016c). In addition, the motivation of employees has been challenged by the generally low wages for PES frontline staff and the daily pressures associated with providing client services. Table 3.1 provides information on the overall case load of PES personnel between 2010 and 2015. The number of unemployed people per counsellor is clearly increasing, which confirms stakeholder feedback that was provided during the OECD study visit. Concrete measures have recently been taken by the government to strengthen the quality of PES counselling, especially for programmes which aim to assist youth (see Box 3.1).

Table 3.1. **Number of unemployed in Slovenia, case-loads per counselling personnel**

	Registered unemployed	Number of unemployed per counselling staff		Time* per unemployed person (in hours)	
		Unemployed per all counselling staff	Excluding project financed counselling staff	All counselling in hours	Excluding project financed counselling staff
2010	100 504	384	463	3,3	3,9
2011	110 692	379	448	3,4	4
2012	110 183	361	424	3,6	4,2
2013	119 827	394	463	3,3	3,8
2014	120 109	406	479	3,2	3,7
2015	107 412	385	531	3,4	3,9

* Time refers to all PES activities per unemployed person per year, both individual and group work, allocation of candidates to jobs, monitoring allocation as well as working with employers.

Source: SORS (2015).

> **Box 3.1. Strengthening PES counselling activities for the young**
>
> The PES has strengthened its counselling work with youth. Between 2014 and 2015, 68 new and specially trained counsellors were employed by PES in order to strengthen the counselling activities for youth, increase the quality of counselling and increase the efficiency of career guidance with the final goal of realising the Youth Guarantee. The increased number of counsellors allowed the PES to sustain case-loads and increase the counselling time per unemployed. The unemployed were able to obtain quality information and counselling based on their interests and needs and without the need to make appointments. Without the additional counsellors, the case-load per counsellor would be significantly higher, implying less counselling as well as less customised services.
>
> These counsellors have an opportunity to get to know their clients better and create alternative employment goals. In many cases, youth have been able to reach their goals primarily due to the strengthened support and goal-oriented counselling. The primary purpose of the project was to work efficiently with youth and improve their employment prospects. To achieve that, counsellors try to consider young people's values, lifestyle and perceptions.
>
> The counselling activities were thereby incorporating more elements of life-long career planning. Local PES directors were also invited to evaluate the impact of the strengthened counselling teams on the 1) use of new, innovative approaches in co-operation with employers, 2) use of new and modern communication channels, 3) creativity in career

> Box 3.1. **Strengthening PES counselling activities for the young** (*cont.*)
>
> guidance, 4) implementation of fresh ideas and approaches, 5) feedback from the unemployed, especially regarding the communication, and 6) considering the needs of the young.
>
> The evaluation revealed that the increase in the number of counselling staff and the specialised training, significantly improved the quality of PES services. The general satisfaction with PES services increased, and youth expressed more satisfaction than the average recipient of PES services. The new counsellors and their innovative work methods, energy and their desire to tailor their services improved the quality of work at PES. The results support the view that the measures within the "Youth Guarantee" were successful and also improved the position of the young in the labour market.
>
> Between 2016 and 2022, the PES will implement a similar project to target the long-term unemployed, one of the most problematic groups within the labour market. The PES will further increase the number of counselling staff, which will be specially trained for the work with disadvantaged groups in the labour market and equipped with motivation techniques.

Policy co-ordination, policy integration and co-operation with other sectors

Generally, collaboration and communication at the regional and local level could be stronger and more active in all policy areas. Communication between the employment and training sectors at the regional or local level is not institutionalised. The majority of communication is sporadic and ad-hoc and there is no formal mechanism to ensure joined-up working across policy portfolios. While the recent process that led to the establishment of a National Skills Strategy in Slovenia shows that it is possible to bring together stakeholders from different ministries, authorities and sectors around strategic goals, the culture and practice of stakeholder engagement remains weak in Slovenia, including in the policy area of skills (OECD, forthcoming, 2017a).

Regional development agencies are active in organising collaboration between different stakeholders to prepare regional development plans. This includes the training sector, the PES, and employers. A development board, which includes the PES, meets regularly to discuss development priorities for the region. The outcomes from the development boards are summarised in extensive regional development programmes, including the *Regional Development Plan for the Drava region* (Regionalni razvojni program za podravsko razvojno regijo, 2015) and *Regional Development Plan for the South-East Slovenia region* (Regionalni razvojni program Jugovzhodne Slovenije 2014-20, 2015).

Regional development plans are prepared in collaboration with local stakeholders but there sometimes appears to be a divide between the regional level plans and those articulated at the national level. Also, there are often local development agendas prepared by different institutions (e.g. the development agency and the local municipality) which may have different strategic focuses. Furthermore, the new regional development projects (in the new operational plan of financing development from the EU sources) are more focused on requiring co-operation from local stakeholders. The new Smart Specialisation Strategy of Slovenia has been well received by local stakeholders and is expected to better integrate employment and economic development objectives.

Co-operation among municipalities is challenging because of the number of administrative areas that exist in Slovenia, as well as the uneven financial and human resources across municipalities. The number of municipalities in Slovenia has grown over the last 20 years, in contrast to the trend in most other OECD countries. Many municipalities are too small to provide public services efficiently and municipal mergers and financial incentives for inter-municipal co-operation should be a policy priority (OECD, 2015a). The new Operational Programme will focus on stimulating co-operation by awarding additional points in public tenders in case of "co-operative" projects among municipalities.

Co-operation between economic development policies and the PES can be hampered because of the organisational structures in Slovenia. For example, regions are defined on a NUTS3 basis, but the regional organisation of the PES does not align with these administrative boundaries. For example, Kočevje is a municipality facing a number of labour market challenges and is located in the South-East Slovenia region, but it falls under the Central Slovenia region in terms of the PES organisational structure. While Kočevje has stronger economical and geographical linkages to the Central Slovenian region than South-East Slovenia, it has significantly different local development and labour market issues.

The regional organisation of the PES also presents challenges in terms of policy planning. As an example, Kočevje is less developed with a vastly different labour market to Ljubljana, but both areas fall under the same PES regional office. From the perspective of economic development administration, Kočevje is part of the South-East Slovenia region, while Ljubljana is part of Central Slovenia.

In both case study regions, the PES has active communication and co-ordination with employers. At the national level, the PES is a member of the social partnership and is therefore involved in significant labour market changes that require co-ordination among the social partners. At the regional level, the PES is also a member of the development boards, which bring together a number of local stakeholders. The results from the OECD questionnaire to local PES offices also demonstrate that high emphasis is placed on reaching out to employers (see Table 3.2). Local and regional PES offices reported more collaboration with employers and chambers of commerce than with other stakeholders.

Table 3.2. **PES collaboration with other stakeholders**

	Most collaboration	Least collaboration
Local PES offices	• Employers and chambers of commerce • Private or public training facilities • Local government	• Slovene human resources and development and scholarship fund • Universities • Specialized industry chambers • Private sector employment agencies • Other NGOs
Regional PES offices	• Employers, associations of employers, chambers of commerce • Vocational schools • Welfare and social integration institutions	• Universities • Slovene human resources and development scholarship fund • Post-secondary schools

Source: OECD Public Employment Services Questionnaire.

Local PES offices provide continuous support to employers through the Offices for Employers, which were opened in 2014. The Offices for Employers offer a number of services, including gathering information about vacancies; professional selection of appropriate and motivated candidates; providing information about the currently available incentives for recruitment and training of new employees; assistance in completing applications and forms, which are required in order to obtain specific services for employers; and information about the legal obligations of the employer after the employment of a new employee (when using services and incentives by PES). If there are no appropriate candidates in the local labour market, the PES provides the following services to employers:

- Appropriate candidates can be sought throughout Slovenia and the EU area through the internal PES database;
- The PES can organise special presentations of vacancies available and companies to unemployed candidates with the appropriate knowledge, skills and motivation necessary.
- The PES can co-finance the training of motivated candidates;
- Available candidates can be trained according to special educational programmes that provide specific professional knowledge, skills and competences required from companies;
- The PES can provide special grants for certain groups of the unemployed;
- The PES can organise mini employment fairs to bring unemployed and employed individuals together. Short interviews can be organised with candidates to help companies select new employees.

In both case study areas, the PES works well with not-for-profit and adult-education institutions (see Box 3.2). In this context, a number of programmes (financed largely from the European Social Fund) were implemented, including training to improve basic computer skills and language skills, as well as special programmes for disadvantaged groups (e.g. Roma and immigrants). This co-operation was also acknowledged by the municipalities and local development institutions.

> **Box 3.2. Example of adult education centres: *Razvojno-izobraževalni centre (RIC) Novo mesto***
>
> RIC Novo mesto is a public institution for adult education. Traditionally, the RIC (and predecessors) were an important adult education facility, primarily offering primary school for adults, different secondary programmes for adults and language courses.
>
> They co-operated with PES to offer skills development opportunities to the unemployed. After 1990, the centre expanded its activities to a number of other activities. Besides formal educational programmes, which include primary school for adults as well as secondary vocational programmes for other occupations (e.g. salesmen, commercial technicians), the RIC also provides general programmes for disadvantaged groups. These programmes include project learning for young adults, study groups, training to be more successful in life, language courses, programmes for active citizenship, programmes for older adults, special needs' individuals and Roma.
>
> They also provide computer programmes for the general public as well as a self-study area and counselling services. Counselling for adults is a special programme (ISIO centres) that is offered in RIC to support adults in all stages of education and learning. In addition, the RIC also provides European Business Competence License (EBCL) certificate training to help participants achieve an internationally recognised certificate of business skills. RIC also works with the corporate sector and prepares special computer and language programmes that are tailored to the needs of companies.
>
> RIC is just one example of an adult education centre or "peoples' university". *Ljudska Univerza Kočevje, Zavod za izobraževanje in kulturo, Črnomelj, Center za izobraževanje in kulturo Trebnje, Andragoški zavod Maribor, Ljudska univerza Ptuj, Ljudska univerza Ormož* are also examples of similar institutions providing similar services at local area.
>
> In general, adult education centres are important local stakeholders due to their specialisation in the field of life-long learning and work with different disadvantaged groups.

> Box 3.2. **Example of adult education centres:** *Razvojno-izobraževalni centre (RIC) Novo mesto* (cont.)
>
> Their focus on different formal programmes place emphasis on general competences (e,g, literacy, communication, computer, and presentation skills), which are extremely important for labour market success. Often, these skills are neglected in skills development programmes in Slovenia.
>
> *Source:* RIC (2015), ZLUS (2015).

Evidence based policy making

In a recent OECD review of the Slovenian Skills Strategy (OECD, 2017), it is noted that the skills assessment and anticipation system is not sufficiently developed. This means that decision makers at all levels do not have access to the appropriate information that would enable them to respond to changing conditions in the labour market. The main source of information that is at their disposal concerns occupations that are currently in high demand. But no system is in place to anticipate future skills needs. In addition, little information is available on the supply of skills, which means that imbalances on the market for skills cannot be easily detected. This lack of quality labour market information also hampers career guidance services.

Local stakeholders rely on available data in the development of employment and economic development strategies. Data can be sourced from Eurostat, which offers some regional data, as well as the Statistical Office of Slovenia. Data at the municipal level is harder to obtain due to general availability and in some cases confidentiality issues (firm level, individual data for further analysis). Regional data can be found at SORS Maps and website, where more popular data are collected at the regional and municipal level. More detailed data is also available in the SI-Stat Data portal database. When available, data are often used in programme and policy development when available.

The PES also has a rich internal database of all unemployed, which they actively analyse for internal purposes. They also have partial coverage of the demand for workers, based on reported vacancies. However, as of 2012, the reporting of vacancies is no longer obligatory, so coverage is only partial. An interesting project within the PES involved forecasting employment, which looks not only at general trends but the types of skills required of future jobs (see Box 3.3).

Alongside official statistical sources (SORS, Eurostat), data on the regional labour market situation can be partially obtained from the Centre of Social Security and local employers that provide information to the PES. Also, more detailed data on employment could be obtained for empirical research from firm-level data, which are available to selected institutions via AJPES (The Agency of the Republic of Slovenia for Public Legal Records and Related Services). Data are also subject to data-protection clauses. Other stakeholders, such as the chambers of commerce and development agencies, do not regularly conduct labour market analysis due to resource issues. There could be an opportunity to merge chambers together at the local level and give them more resources to conduct labour market analysis and forecasting on a sector basis.

Although data are available and are being used when preparing policies, more could be done to better utilise information in the evaluation of programmes and policies. Previous OECD work on Slovenia has highlighted the importance of creating a system of

> **Box 3.3. "Forecasting employment needs"**
>
> The PES in 2014 established the "Forecasting employment" (*Napovednik zaposlovanja*) project, which gathers information about the plans of the employers to employ in the next 6 months, the main occupations they will employ and the problems they are facing in employing (which occupations and what skills are missing).
>
> The results of the survey show that technical profiles are most in demand. Through several rounds of this survey, it has been found that welders, metal workers, drivers, elementary workers and electricians have been the most desired profiles. The results also show that 22% of Slovenian companies encountered problems when trying to find suitable candidates, which rises to 25.6%, 31.8% and 31% in Maribor, Ptuj and Novo mesto respectively. Generally, bigger companies had more problems when looking for suitable candidates, but they also have more vacancies and often seek very specific profiles.
>
> *Source:* Employment service of the Republic of Slovenia, Napovednik zaposlovanja, 2015.

independent evaluations for active labour market programmes to improve their efficiency (OECD, 2015c). Furthermore, there is no systematic data-collection gathered for travel-to-work areas, regions and municipalities. Data on the basis of travel-to-work areas are not available through SORS.

Due to the size of the economy, research at the national level can also provide relevant results for local communities, either because the topic is generally relevant and the whole economy is analysed or a regional focus is taken. Such analysis is often conducted in co-operation with academia. Through public calls, the government and the Slovenia Research Agency regularly provide funding for either "targeted research projects" or applied research. Often, development and labour market issues are financed.

Theme 2: Adding value through skills

Figure 3.4. **Dashboard results for adding value through skills**

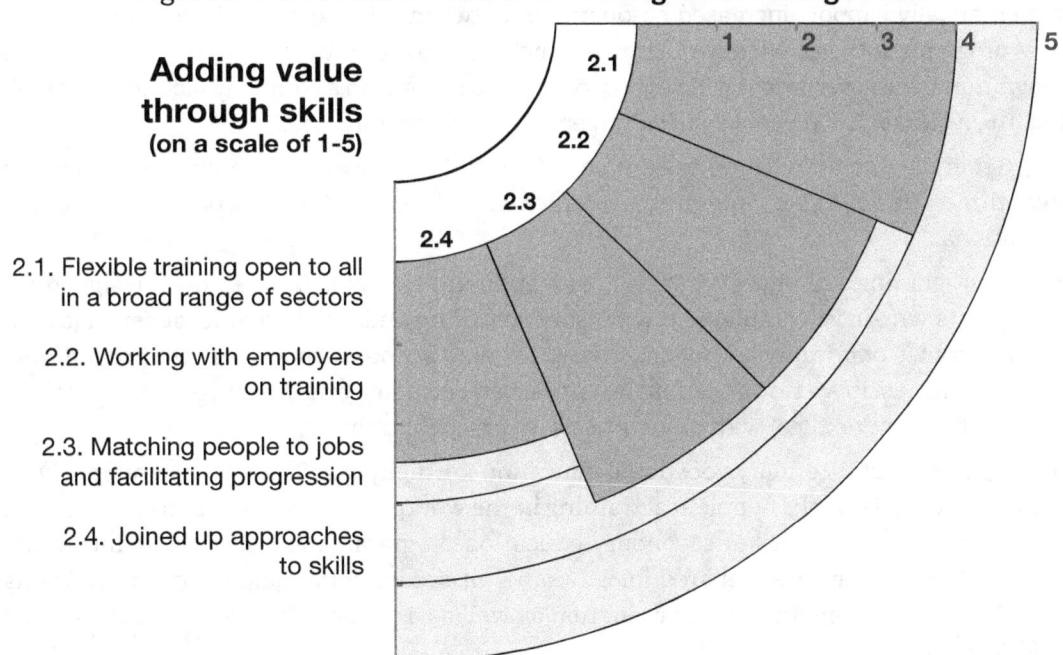

Flexible training is open to all in a broad range of sectors

The OECD dashboard results show that Slovenia is doing well in terms of providing accessible training in a broad range of sectors. In general, there is a strong network of primary and secondary schools, as well as higher degree programmes (e.g. the University in Maribor in Drava region, the University in Novo mesto in the South-East Slovenia region, as well as higher degree programmes offered through vocational education centres). Yet while recent governments have given a clear priority to improving the employability of young individuals by promoting life-long career orientation, upskilling opportunities for older workers has tended to be somewhat neglected (OECD, 2017b forthcoming).

From the primary level, students develop basic skills and higher level generic skills (including networking, communication, leadership, innovation and problem solving). Some schools even offer entrepreneurship education from a young age, depending on the availability of such electives. These skills are then further strengthened in secondary education and vocational education. In some national vocational qualification programmes, such as care-taker, these skills are a mandatory part of the curriculum. For adults, generic skills can be upgraded through the not-for-profit sector or adult education centres. Developing entrepreneurial skills among the Slovenian population would be all the more beneficial to the economy that the country currently lacks the ability to effectively translate its quality research and development activities into innovative products and services that can be commercialised in both national and international markets (OECD, forthcoming, 2017b).

Vocational schools or school centres (which are comprised of several different schools) offer a number of different programmes in vocational education (e.g. *Tehniški šolski cente Maribor, Srednješolski centre Ptuj, Šolski centre Novo mesto, Srednješolski centre Črnomelj, Srednja šola in gimnazija Kočevje*). These institutions offer formal educational programmes for youth and adults. They also offer higher educational programmes and special training for companies – some have specific inter-company training centres (MIC – Medpodjetniški izobraževalni cente). Their activities are often supported by local partners – for example, the higher education unit in Maribor's training centre has 84 partners. The PES will systematically support increased co-operation between MICs and employers through the new programme "I can, because I know", which aims to re-train job-seekers. Through this programme, the government will support on-the job training in a company (about 104 hours). In 2016, a total of 1 600 people will be targeted in such programmes.

Generally, there are three basic types of secondary vocational training programmes: two, three and four year programmes, which can all lead to university under specified conditions.

- The programmes of short vocational education are two year programmes designed for students who have completed compulsory schooling and finished at least seven (out of nine) grades of primary school or finished primary school with an adapted programme. Programmes in various professions are offered (e.g. engineering, construction, biotechnology, textiles) with an emphasis on practical training.
- Programmes of secondary vocational education normally take three years and involve a minimum of 24 weeks of practical training in the workplace. Anyone who has completed basic education or a lower secondary education programme can join this educational track. Programmes are prepared for a number of occupational fields and training ends with a final written and oral examination as well as a presentation of a product/service (CPI, 2015).

- General and technical programmes are also intended for students who have completed basic education or lower secondary education or short term vocational programmes, but they last four years rather than three. They provide vocational training, but also provide a pathway into higher professional education (CPI, 2015).

Adults with vocational skills only have limited opportunities to retrain throughout their working lives. Schools do offer diploma programmes (upper secondary or higher education) as well as shorter modular courses, national vocational qualifications programmes, or trainings prepared in co-operation with local companies and/or the local PES, but this is not an adequate way of helping older workers to upskill or retrain for new occupations (OECD, 2017b forthcoming). Financial support to undertake higher education courses are often reserved to students aged under 25. As a result, only 6% of new entrants in such courses were aged over 24 in 2015, compared to 18% on average in OECD countries, and the enrolment rate for the population aged 30 to 64 halved between 2005 and 2014 (OECD, 2017b forthcoming). The fact that part-time courses, which are likely to be more attractive for those in employment, are often undersubscribed may also be the consequence of a financial support system that does not favour such courses.

Some initiatives have been taken to encourage retraining of older workers. In early 2017, the national government has announced the creation of a new programme entitled "Comprehensive Support to Companies for Active Aging of Employees" which will provide skills upgrading opportunities to 12 500 older workers by 2022. In Bela Krajina, the Akrapovič exhaust pipes company set up a training programme through a partnership with the local PES office. In addition to the programmes for adults offered through secondary school centres, training is also available through adult educational centres ("peoples' universities"). As "formal programmes" are broadly available in secondary school centres, the importance of these institutions is primarily in providing training for different skills, such as ICT, communication skills and language training.

Schools and the Ministry of Education are able to suggest the development of new programmes (national curriculum) that provide an official diploma. National vocational qualifications (NVQ) are defined by law and provide official national certificates of qualifications. If the qualification is needed by a specific branch – provided that a similar one does not exist – the CPI typically prepares occupational standard and the assessment catalogue of the qualification within six months.

Looking specifically at the case study areas, schools in both areas offer a number of programmes in various technical and scientific fields. In South-East Slovenia, the biggest secondary educational centre is in Novo mesto but there are also smaller centres in municipalities such as Kočevje and Črnomelj. The agricultural education centre "Grm" in Novo mesto is one of the strongest centres in this field nationally (see Box 3.4). Similarly, the biggest centre of education in the Drava region is in the region's capital, Maribor, but smaller municipalities including Ptuj and Ruše also have training centres. While provision is generally adequate in the larger centres, smaller educational centres face more challenges, particularly related to engaging a sufficient number of students to reach the "critical mass" needed to offer courses, and working with local employers (e.g. related to work-based learning).

Compared to other EU28 countries, Slovenia performs slightly better than average in the participation of unemployed and low-skilled workers in training (see Figure 3.5).

> **Box 3.4. Centre Grm, Centre of biotechnology and tourism**
>
> Grm Novo mesto is an education and development centre that specialises in the fields of biotechnology (agriculture, horticulture, food and nutrition, veterinary medicine, forestry and hunting, nature conservation, environmental protection, sports and recreation in the countryside, social welfare in rural areas) and tourism (hospitality, gastronomy, hotel business, rural and urban tourism, sport and recreation).
>
> Grm Novo mesto is comprised of several educational institutions: Agricultural School Grm and Biotechnical School, Secondary School for Hospitality and Tourism, Vocational College, Student Hostel, Business Educational Centre with the school farms, food processing plants and the Culinary House, a restaurant in Novo mesto. Agricultural School Grm and the Biotechnical School are the oldest programmes of the school, which was established in 1886. In 2000, the school started a higher educational programme, which today offers three programmes: countryside and landscape management, nature protection, and catering and tourism. The centre also includes an R&D Institute, which founded the Higher School of Rural Management in Novo mesto.
>
> The school is actively involved in agriculture and tourism in the region and engages its alumni through seminars and events, including opportunities for lifelong learning. The centre also stimulates co-operation between individuals. Finally, from the first year of education, the school actively promotes entrepreneurship in agriculture and tourism. As such, the centre is an active and important actor in regional (and national) agriculture and tourism.
>
> *Source:* Interviews with Centre Grm undertaken for LEED, 2015.

Figure 3.5. **Participation rate in education and training (previous 4 weeks), aged 18-64, 2015**

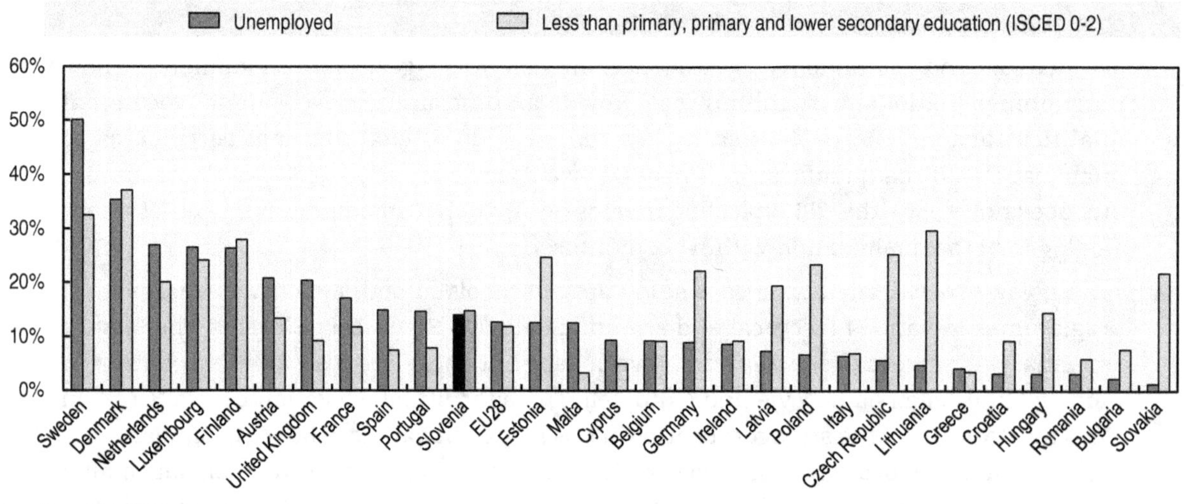

Source: Eurostat (2017a).

The PES subsidises training to help unemployed people obtain additional qualifications. Decisions about training are based on personal employment plans. Generally, unemployed persons can enrol in training as long as it aligns with their personal employment plan and is supported by PES. These programmes tend to be short (e.g. national vocational qualification, e.g. 60-150 hours, with different combinations of practical and theoretical parts). Longer or more formal programmes for diplomas are less commonly supported by PES.

Employers that offer on-the-job training for the "hard to employ" (for up to 3 months) are eligible for a subsidy after the training is completed. In addition a new instrument, "Zmorem, ker znam", was launched in 2016 with the aim of increasing co-operation between employers, education and training organisations, and PES.

Working with employers on training

While no exact measure is available, a number of indicators can be useful in determining the extent to which training is aligned to employer needs. In 2015, 24.3% of employers faced difficulties in finding suitable candidates whereas in large firms, the share was 33% (Manpower, 2015). In an analysis conducted by the PES, over 75% of employers reported that candidates are primarily missing occupational or vocational-specific skills. Employers specifically report challenges with finding candidates with organisational, team-working, and problem solving skills (see Figure 3.6). In another study of Slovenian employers who recruited higher education graduates, 62% reported being "somewhat" satisfied with their sector specific skills, while 15% reported being "rather not satisfied or not satisfied at all" and 20% reported being "very satisfied (EU Barometer, 2010).

Figure 3.6. **Skills that the candidates are missing according to local employers, 2015**

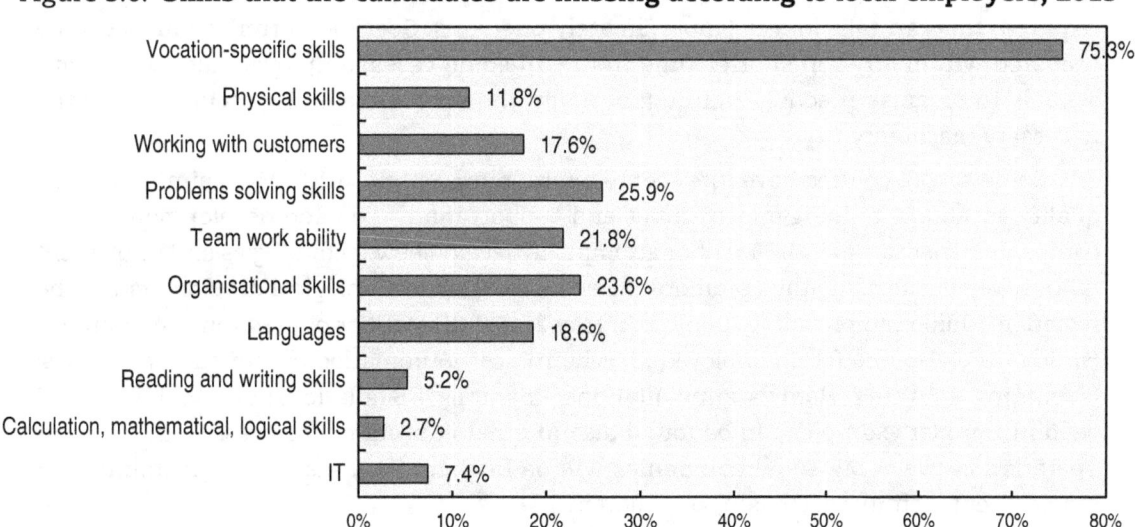

Source: ESS (2015).

The OECD distributed a questionnaire to local employment offices to ascertain their view on the responsiveness of training to local employer needs. In the view of representatives of local public employment services, training provided through the formal education system is least likely to be aligned with employer needs, while training within Active Labour Market Policy (ALMP) measures are more positively assessed (see Figure 3.7). In one survey, 38% of Slovenian employers reported that they have never co-operated with higher education institutes to discuss curriculum design and study programmes (EU Barometer, 2010).

However, it should be acknowledged that some schools work very well with employers. Based on the Law on Vocational and Professional Education (*Zakon o poklicnem in strokovnem izobraževanju*, 2006), 20% of the vocational curriculum is left "open" for local actors to prepare, often in co-operation with local employers. Employers can also suggest new vocational qualifications or even educational programmes. If a new programme is

Figure 3.7. **The responsiveness of Public Employment Services to local employer needs**

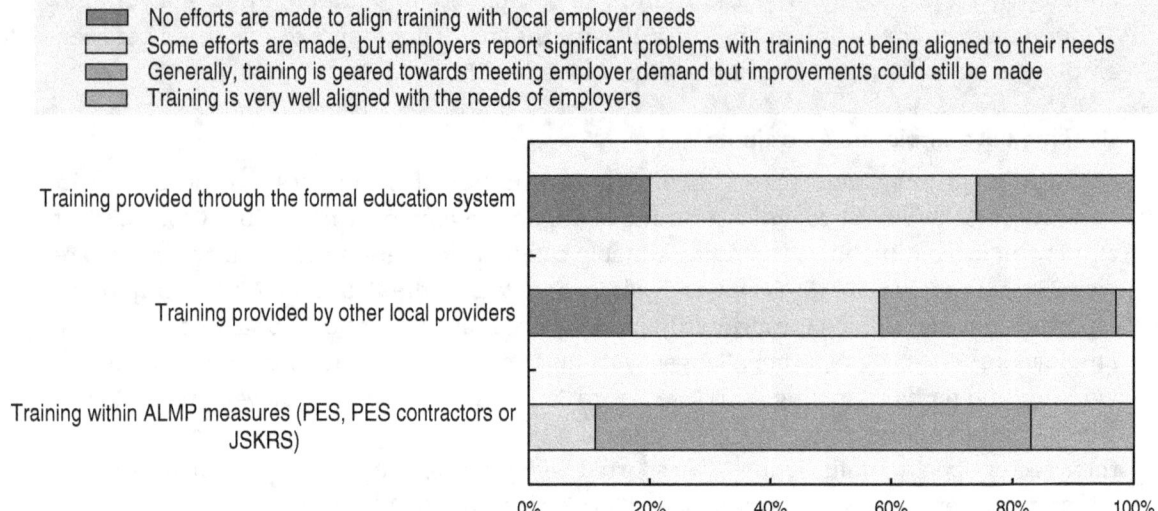

Source: OECD Public Employment Services Questionnaire.

required, this can take longer (approximately one year). Special shorter modules can be prepared within an even shorter time frame. In some cases, employers also work with schools to organise practical training, or equip the school's learning facilities with the necessary machinery.

Some school centres have inter-company training centres (MIC). MICs aim to develop quality vocational training opportunities and support innovation and development within companies. For example, MIC Maribor attempts to develop new technologies and implement innovative activities and thus promote the economic and technological development of the region in addition to providing training. In May 2015, MIC Maribor offered four programmes (which were also free for unemployed): Mechatronics – Automation of industrial processes; Machining – Turning; Hardware Installations – Sanitary Installations; and Welding – TIG welding. Similar examples can be found also in other educational centres. From 2016, co-operation between MICs and companies will be further stimulated through training for employment instrument ("Znam, ker zmorem").

Employers can also directly engage in vocational education design. For example, a large employer in the South-East Slovenia region suggested the development of a programme on "industrial pharmaceuticals". While this plan was not implemented, they are still very active in education and training. They developed six internationally certified national vocational qualifications that are customised to their specific needs. The company also has a practical and co-operative relationship with the pharmaceutical faculty in Ljubljana, where employees teach classes at the university.

Workplace training and apprenticeships

Approximately 68% of employers in Slovenia offer continuing vocational education training (CVET) to their employees, slightly above the average of 66% in EU28 countries. The most common factors influencing the provision of employer-sponsored training in Slovenia were training being too expensive (43%), a major training effort already undertaken in the previous year (29%), or a focus on initial vocational training rather than CVET (19%). Only 10%

of employers that offer training reported that public measures had an impact on their CVET plans, compared to an estimated EU28 average of 26% (Eurostat, 2016).

Larger employers invest significantly in human resource development. For example, one large Slovenian company located in South-East Slovenia provides an average of 55 hours of training to employees annually, which covers general (IT, languages, etc.) as well as occupational-specific skills. There are also a number of large companies in both case study areas that invest in training, primarily because they are developing new products. Typically, these programmes are conducted through on-the-job training, but employers are beginning to invest more in official programmes for diplomas. On the other hand, smaller companies find it much harder to invest in specific training for both organisational and financial reasons.

Apprenticeships are not currently available in Slovenia, but are in the process of being launched (e.g. CPI, 2014). A pilot programme for the establishment of a dual apprenticeship-training system, co-financed by the Ministry of Education and the European Social Fund, will be launched for six to eight industries in 2017-18. While practical on the job training is already part of other vocational programmes, the time spent in practical training will be increased to at least 50% of the programme curriculum in the new system. Some employed and unemployed adults will also be able to participate in the system. An important role will be given to the Chamber of Commerce which will be involved at various stages.

The Law on vocational and professional education (*Zakon o poklicnem in strokovnem izobraževanju* [Vocational and Professional Education Act], 2006) provides the framework to the preparation of vocational and professional programmes, and on the job training represents the biggest share of two year vocational programmes. In three year programmes, it is 24-weeks long, while in four year programmes, it takes 4-10 weeks.

Matching people to jobs

Career planning usually begins in basic education and continues to the secondary level. Counsellors in basic education conduct career and vocational counselling from the sixth grade, while elective or additional courses also provide insight and guidance to students with regard to their interests and future vocational opportunities.

Many career activities take place at the secondary school level. For example, the Grm centre of agriculture and tourism in South-East Slovenia has developed a programme of "individual counselling", where both parents (often farm owners) and students are invited to identify a specialisation and a desired career path early in secondary education. Through later school work, pupils prepare an entrepreneurial idea and plan. Many succeed in starting companies before they even finish school.

However, there are a number of challenges related to career guidance within the short and technical vocational education system. Short vocational education is generally viewed as a "second choice" educational pathway. Similar to other OECD countries, parents in Slovenia generally have a negative attitude towards short vocational education, which may help to explain why the university enrolment rate is among highest in the EU. There is a perception that pupils from short vocational or vocational technical schools were unable to go to university, and that these programmes can be completed more easily. In Bela Krajina, for example, schools have attempted to change this perception by inviting employers to information days and connecting employers and parents in eight and ninth grades to attract them to their vocational and technical programmes.

Career support for older works is less organised and depends on the individual situation (e.g. whether they are employed or unemployed). General counselling is available through ISIO centres for self-learning. Career guidance is also available at the GENEP centres, while adult education centres and the not-for profit sector conduct career counselling. For example in the South-east Slovenia region, RIC as well as other adult education centres and the peoples' universities" are active in consulting and are also involved with employers. A successful project was ZaTE that brought together different labour market stakeholders. There is also some support for professional development and development of career ladders for low-qualified workers. This is primarily through the activities of PES, "peoples' universities", and the not-for profit sector.

In order to improve the responsiveness of the VET system to the needs of the labour market, incentives have recently been put in place to encourage students to choose VET courses that correspond to occupations for which there are labour shortages. In 2015, a 'Scholarship for Shortage Occupations' scheme was established with a monthly stipend of EUR 100. The Ministry of Labour, Family and Social Affairs determines the occupations that are covered by the scheme after consultation with social partners.

At university level, more could be done to provide graduates with the skills that are needed in the labour market. For example, the funding system for universities could provide better incentives to align curricula to employer skills demands (OECD, 2017b). The fact that universities are currently paid a lump sum paid per students enrolled incentivises establishments to prioritise quantity over quality. A different funding system that would be partly based on the labour market performance of graduates could help to improve the alignment between university curricula and labour market demands. Better links with industry could also contribute to improve the responsiveness of higher education institutions. Although there are plenty of evidence of top-tier Slovenian firms engaging with training and research institutions, through scholarship schemes for example (OECD, 2015b), employers do not have the possibility to influence higher education curricula and are generally not represented on boards of management. Finally, the lack of internationalisation of higher education institutions may also hinder their ability to respond to new technological trends and to provide graduates with the skills that are needed to succeed on the global marketplace for jobs and skills (OECD, 2017b).

Activation and job-matching through PES

At the PES, all registered unemployed people receive counselling. The PES develops individual employment plans that consider the individuals experience, education, and labour market experience in order to find the best possible job match. Counselling is typically the only instrument used in the first three months of jobseeking, as the unemployed are expected first to show that they are actively searching for work. Jobseekers with specific needs may immediately receive additional support (for example, early school leavers can receive support through PUM). Yet, as a whole, Slovenia spends relatively little on active labour market programmes (ALMP) as a share of GDP in comparison to the OECD average.

Given that it is generally easier to find a new job while still being in employment, it would be beneficial to incentivise workers who are at risk of being displaced to engage in activation programmes before they lose their job, for example through mandatory registration with ESS (OECD, 2016c). Yet, at present, there are no procedures in place for early activation of potential job-seekers and ESS staff are not encouraged to provide job-search assistance to workers who have been notified termination of their employment

Figure 3.8. **Public expenditure on active labour market programmes (as % or GDP), 2013**

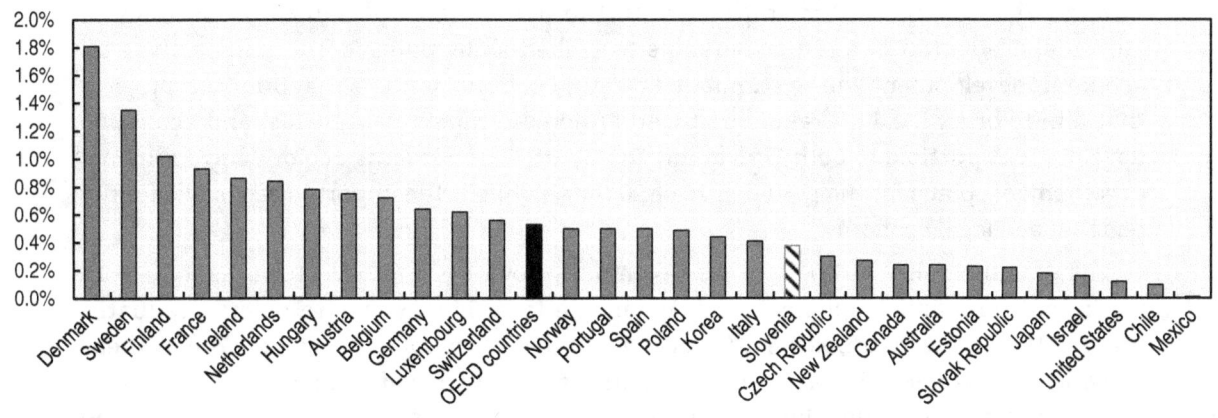

Source: OECD (2017c).

(OECD, 2017b). In addition, activation programmes that target displaced workers could be extended and improved as they currently do not benefit from sufficient dedicated resources and coverage (OECD, 2016c).

When employers approach the PES in search of a specific profile, the PES can use an internal database that provides data on all registered unemployed people across Slovenia to find a list of suitable candidates. Generally, both the candidate and the firm prefer to find matches that do not require long commutes, particularly because travel costs are covered by employers in Slovenia. Nonetheless, firms report that individuals have become more willing to commute longer distances to work following the economic crisis, which is also evident from the regional and municipal migration data.

Local recruitment challenges are usually firm-specific- due to the size of economy it is hard to speak of any regional specialisation in terms of large clusters that would require a more systematic approach or a strategy. In such cases, either the PES assists local employers or the firm seeks other assistance through vocational education or internal training programmes. Through the Regional Scholarship scheme, companies also provide scholarships in order to encourage students to work with them after finishing a specific programme.

There are also mechanisms to validate skills obtained informally. Individuals can demonstrate proficiency by passing a national vocational test and receiving a public document – certificate on national vocational qualification as regulated by National Professional Qualifications Act. There are a vast number of fields where such national vocational qualifications exist and these qualifications are revised every five years. They can also be expanded with pressure from local companies and other stakeholders.

Joined up approaches to skills

Local stakeholders recognise the importance of harnessing and attracting talent, and references to skills can be found in the relevant economic development strategies. While a systematic and co-ordinated approach does not exist, some action is being taken by individual actors. In South-East Slovenia, companies such as Krka, Revoz and Adria Mobile attract talent to the region. Local stakeholders also recognise the benefits of domestic employers, especially within higher-value added sectors that focus on R&D activities and generally stimulate better economic development opportunities.

Co-operation at the local level to bring together skills and perspectives on economic development is expected to improve with the new Smart Specialisation Strategy of Slovenia. Co-operation and partnerships to embed skills policies into perspectives on economic development will be stimulated through national tenders that prioritise projects that aim to bring local stakeholders together across employment, skills, and economic development portfolios. Both Drava and the South-East Slovenia regions have regional developments plans for the period of 2014-20 that highlight the importance of skills for the regional and local economy.

The municipality of Kočevje has taken an innovative approach towards joined-up working. It prepares "diploma" evenings in the local library, where recent graduates present their work to employers. Several graduates have obtained work through these activities. The municipality also aims to retain keep quality labour, and involves employers in the preparation of development programmes. The municipality also stresses the importance of human resources to potential investors.

According to the Regional Development Plan of the Drava region 2014-20, the priority areas in which skills will have to be developed are: management skills, communication skills, foreign languages with a focus on English and German, and information and communication technology. The growing demand for professionals from information technology could be strengthened by creating closer linkages between academic centres and companies and promoting education in the field of information technology. The Regional Development Plan also acknowledges the importance of innovation that encourages the development and creation of high-value businesses. Furthermore, there is a focus on entrepreneurship and supporting the development of SMEs.

According to the Regional Development Plan of the South-East Slovenia region 2014-20, informal and non-formal education is needed in order to increase employment opportunities through the acquisition of general and professional competences, taking into account development policies and projections, such as the expected increase in green jobs. The plan also points to the importance of boosting entrepreneurship skills and Information and Communication Technology (ICT). The plan notes that intercompany training centres (MICs) should have a stronger role in the implementation of training programmes for the employed and unemployed. It also stresses the importance of harmonising vocational education with the needs of the economy and increasing the overall enrolment in short vocational and technical education.

Theme 3: Targeting policy to local employment sectors and investing in quality jobs

Figure 3.9. **Dashboard results for targeting policy to local employment sectors and investing in quality jobs**

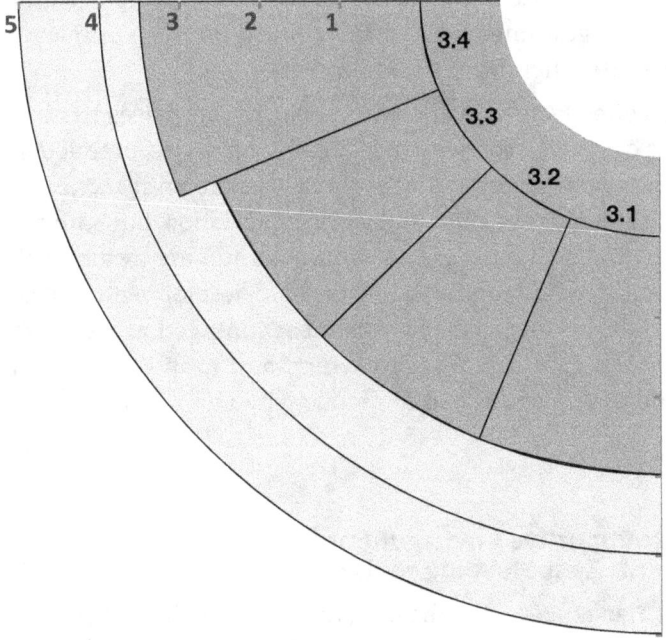

Targeting policy
(on a scale of 1-5)

3.1. Relevance of provision to important local employment sectors and global trends and challenges

3.2. Work with employers on skills utilisation and productivity

3.3. Promotion of skills for entrepreneurship

3.4. Economic development promotes quality jobs for local people

Relevance of provision to important local employment sectors and global trends and challenges

Regional development programmes in both case study regions acknowledge the problems of population ageing and sustainability but planning is somewhat ad-hoc. Many OECD countries use sophisticated skills forecasting models, which provide a breakdown of trends by sector and level of education over the long-term. However, no such planning exists in Slovenia. In Slovenia, IMAD (Institute for Economic Research and Development) carries out short-term planning twice annually, which provides data on overall employment and unemployment numbers. However, forecasting over the long-term is not done. An analysis of skills planning at the firm level also showed that companies plan poorly for the future, with relatively little attention paid to firm needs a year or more in the future (Pahor et al., 2012).

Some efforts are underway to take global trends into account through policies and programmes. For example, during the OECD study visit, local stakeholders stressed that the new EU operational programme funding will stimulate green jobs. Cohesion funding will be used to promote the "green economy", including funding for jobs in water safety, water quality, waste water, energy efficiency, and transport. In all these areas, green jobs are emerging. For 2015-16, a plan has been developed through a partnership between the Ministry of Environment and the Ministry of Education to promote greater inclusion of green topics into education programmes and curricula. The training sector also actively incorporates green skills into their programmes. For example, the Centre Grm (highlighted earlier) offers a programme in environmental engineering that analyses sustainability issues and environmentally friendly practices in both agriculture as well as tourism.

Work with employers on assuring decent work and skills utilisation

When implementing active labour market policy, the PES tries to match workers to jobs that ensure stability, and minimise instances of employers taking advantage of training and employment subsidies just to lower their labour cost for the duration of the programme. For example, during the OECD study visit, some local PES offices reported that the subsidised on-the-job training programmes were often abused because employers were not obliged to take on trainees after their training is completed.

The performance of Slovenia in effectively using people's skills in workplaces has been found to be mixed (OECD, 2017). This can have negative consequences on wages, productivity and job satisfaction. Generally, public agencies do not actively co-operate with the private sector to look at issues related to the better use of skills and work organisation, but both case study regions are trying to improve the local business environment and are aware of the importance of increasing the demand for skills to further economic development. Special measures have been introduced that are targeted towards disadvantaged areas. These include special regional plans in both case study areas, which aim to increase overall development and broadly aim to address issues related to productivity and skills utilisation (see Box 3.5).

> **Box 3.5. Creating a supportive environment in the Drava and South-East Slovenia regions**
>
> **The Drava Region Development Plan** stresses that the low productivity of firms is one of the problems in the region, as well as limited R&D expenditure and poor marketing skills. As a result, the penetration of export markets is not as high as it could be given the regional location. The Regional Development Plan calls for the enhancement of the supportive environment, strengthening entrepreneurship, and improving other key competences. Overall, the region plans to support the efficiency of companies, among other measures, by:
>
> **1) Increasing overall competitiveness** by stimulating excellence in research; strengthening the innovation capacity of enterprises, including the creation and transfer of new knowledge and solutions from scientific research and educational institutions in the economy; strengthening the international competitiveness of enterprises and promoting the internationalisation of the economy; attracting new investment from the country and from abroad; investing in the development of a supportive environment, including the development of economic infrastructure; providing support services to new and growing businesses and schemes of financial subsidies to encourage start- ups and social enterprises and co-operatives; investing in ICT development and providing more uniform access broadband networks and e-services; and promoting social entrepreneurship and social innovation.
>
> **2) Improving social cohesion and labour market** by improving the quality of life for individuals and families and increasing social cohesion and social inclusion; increasing social inclusion and quality of life for young people, disadvantaged and vulnerable groups; investing in the further development of educational institutions in order to achieve quality and efficient education and training , including the use of innovative technologies and the establishment of systemic higher education study programmes that facilitate entrepreneurship and knowledge transfer; and increasing the impact of research, development and innovation.
>
> **South-East Slovenia region's** 2014-20 Economic Development Plan aims to support the economy and increase the productivity of firms, creating a better environment for entrepreneurship, and strengthening and better utilising key competences. The plan aims to:

> Box 3.5. **Creating a supportive environment in the Drava and South-East Slovenia regions** *(cont.)*
>
> (Regionalni razvojni program za obdobje 2014-20 v razvojni regiji Jugovzhodna Slovenija, 2015, pp.90-92):
>
> **1) Develop a supportive environment** by ensuring an effective and supportive environment; improving the entrepreneurship climate and better disseminating information on business opportunities; promoting entrepreneurship among young people and other groups; building a better understanding of entrepreneurship as an opportunity; increasing the number of fast-growing firms; and establishing a network of incubators (regional network incubator, incubator network Pokolpje).
>
> **2) Raising the productivity of enterprises:** by providing infrastructure and equipment for the development of start-up business; ensuring the development of economic infrastructure which is suitable for new companies, where priority will be given to business districts close to regional centres or where there is a critical mass of labour and businesses; supporting networking and clustering of businesses and other organisations in the region and beyond; implementing various forms of business advice and training in the agriculture, tourism, forestry, wood, creative and cultural industries and implementing counselling and education in social entrepreneurship and economic democracy; assisting in the restructure of business models; raising the competences of those working in supportive environment; integrating new and existing support services of various institutions (development agencies, business chambers of commerce, chambers of crafts, municipalities, etc.); integrating incubators with networks in neighbouring countries; and scoreboard economic infrastructure (occupancy, infrastructural equipment, checking.
>
> **3) Raising skills in the region in various fields of work:** including enterprises and organisations of the region in international co-operation; increasing co-operation with foreign companies and partners, both in European and other markets; recognising the need for new occupations and competencies; introducing new state-approved programmes to meet the needs of the labour market; raising skill levels; increasing participation in international projects; and applying for international sources of funding, particularly EU funds and programmes.

At the national level, the Smart Specialisation strategy identifies specific sectors as key to the competitive advantage of Slovenia. Measures will be introduced based on this national plan. On a case-by-case approach, special regional and sectoral support can be provided by the investment agency.

Local higher education institutes, inter-company training centres and universities are involved with local community and economic development projects. In Novo mesto, for example, the Faculty for Information Studies obtained a silver medal in 2014-15 for their innovation mScan, a programming solution for capturing and managing paper documents in the cloud. This was developed in co-operation with a local business.

Within agriculture and tourism, Center Grm has a research institute that develops knowledge and promotes the use of applied research. They also have a facility that aims to connect local business and their alumni to spread new trends in the use of technology in the workplace. By doing so, they are promoting knowledge networks to share information on new product and production innovations. In Maribor, the local university has started to look at stronger co-operation with the local business community on issues related to skills use.

Promotion of skills for entrepreneurship

Entrepreneurship is acknowledged in the development plans of both the South-East Slovenia and Drava regions. A previous OECD rapid policy assessment of Slovenia highlighted a number of interesting practices to develop training, coaching and mentorship programmes (OECD, 2015a). These programmes include 'Entrepreneurially Into the World of Business' (Podjetno v svet podjetništva), YES Start, ARTUS, Model M 2014, KonektOn, and EnterYOUTH. Many of these programmes are targeted to highly skilled youth, and there are relatively few programmes that focus on the core working-age population or older workers.

Most entrepreneurship programmes are operated by the PES. One of these programmes was the self-employment programme, which included training; the development of individual business plans; and subsidies to help individuals start businesses (see Box 3.6).

Box 3.6. Self-employment programme by PES and entrepreneurship development

Between 2007 and 2013, the Slovenian PES stimulated employment via a self-employment programme supported by the European Social Fund. In total, 23 316 individuals obtained subsidies for self-employment, but interest in the programme was greater than funding could facilitate. The candidates for the subsidy were required to attend training in basic entrepreneurial skills, then develop and present a business idea. The plans were then assessed for their sustainability.

The measure was successful. More than 94% of the businesses were still in operation after the first year and 85% survived the first two years. Moreover, 19% of the self-employed also became employers themselves and created 2 600 new jobs. The initial target for the inclusion of women was 40%, but over the average inclusion was eventually 41% over the course of the programme.

The majority of the participants in the programme were men from Ljubljana, Maribor and Kranj that had been registered with the Employment Service for approximately 6 months. They were 30 to 39 years old and had secondary education. Approximately 90% of participants began their businesses as sole proprietors in the fields of professional, scientific and technical activities or trade and construction.

However, a critique from social partners was that it encouraged precarious work, and this programme has since been discontinued. As such, there is now a gap in services for unemployed people who wish to start a business but require additional support.

Source: Republic of Slovenia Government Office for Development and European Cohesion Policy (2017).

In 2016, the government launched additional "entrepreneurship" programmes for unemployed women. In the past few years, young women, especially those with a social-science education, have found fewer opportunities in public administration and other fields. Women who have been unemployed for at least three months and with university degrees or higher are now eligible for special "entrepreneurship" programmes conducted over a period of 100 hours. Upon completion, the candidate will be eligible for a EUR 5 000 subsidy over two years in order to support their company.

The OECD's rapid policy assessment of Slovenia notes that entrepreneurship education is generally under-developed and notes that the education sector does not develop creative skills or focus on entrepreneurship and business creation (OECD, 2015a). Generally, entrepreneurship skills are not a part of general training curricula (except in specialised programmes and business schools). Nonetheless, some schools include entrepreneurial topics in their electives and the Ministry of Economic Development and Technology and the Ministry of Education, Science and Sport support a number of initiatives to promote entrepreneurship education. There are examples of secondary vocational and professional schools which place a good deal of emphasis on entrepreneurial skills. For example, Centre Grm includes entrepreneurial skills in all programmes, and students also prepare a plan for their own "job".

In universities, entrepreneurship is present as a standard course in business schools and can also be selected as optional course for some, but not all, other programmes. For example, at the University of Maribor (Drava region), students of electro-technics must select a non-technical elective course in management or a related topic.

Economic development promotes quality jobs for local people

FDI is often used to increase the availability of capital, provide additional technology and skills, improve the quality of jobs and increase economic growth. As such, it can significantly support economic development, especially if there are the desired knock on effects of investors becoming more intertwined with the local economy. Investments from domestic sources can also support economic development. In Bela Krajina, for example, Akrapovič set up a plant in Črnomelj that created new jobs and is expected to significantly boost local economic activity.

Typically, all municipalities try to attract strong investors and employers. For example, in Kočevje (in South-East Slovenia), local authorities and the regional development agency try to attract investors through different activities, such as fairs and disseminating information about potential government incentives, available locations and infrastructure. Kočevje's proximity to Croatia can create challenges, however, as labour costs are comparatively more expensive. Other, more general challenges relate to the limited resources of municipalities and a lack of statutory decision-making authority at the regional level. Other challenges relate to a limited supply of potential investors, meaning that local actors do not have much leeway to "choose" which investors to prioritise.

Quality jobs and employment are part of the strategic development planning in both regions but several obstacles exist in implementation because of insufficient co-operation and "buy-in" among stakeholders. Additionally, given that unemployment is high, much of the focus is on increasing overall employment rather than the quality of jobs. In the Drava region, for example, there has been criticism of new investment from retail chains on the grounds that they do not create quality jobs.

Theme 4: Being inclusive

Figure 3.10. **Dashboard results for being inclusive**

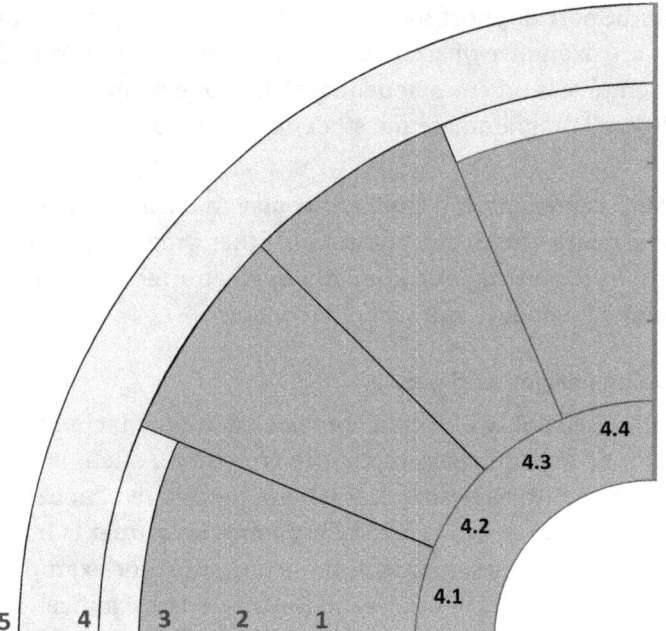

Employment and training programmes are geared to local "at risk" groups

The PES, educational sector, municipalities, not-for-profit sector co-operate in tackling deprivation on both an ad-hoc and systematic basis. In Slovenia, there are a number of at-risk groups that receive significant attention from local PES offices including disabled women, older workers, youth, the Roma, the low skilled, displaced workers, the long-term unemployed, migrants and those from less developed regions. With the support of the national level, special pilot programmes can also be prepared to tackle specific place-based issues.

It has been noted that PES offices have had the tendency to "park" clients that were harder to place by providing less frequent counselling interviews to these jobseekers (OECD, 2016c). This practice was reflected in the fact that claimants experiencing greater labour market barriers were less likely to be referred for ALMPs.

Local PES offices support the inclusion of those that have been out of employment for a longer period. For example, special programmes are available for disabled or older workers, and some programmes are delivered directly to disadvantaged communities. The PES even provides motivational programmes and performs other outreach activities. This "targeted" approach has been successful in the past and the government will continue to support such measures in the 2016-20 period such as entrepreneurship for women, special programmes for youth, as well as programmes for 30-50-year olds.

There is regional variation in disadvantaged groups. In the South-East Slovenia region, the Roma are a focus and receive help through a number of mechanisms. The Adult Education Centre in Kočevje (Ljudska Univerza Kočevje) obtained funding via the Norwegian Financial Mechanism 2009-14 to implement projects for the health of the Roma population. The partners in the project are RIC Novo mesto, Kočevje municipality, Novo mesto

> **Box 3.7. PES for at-risk groups: an example from a programme targeted towards the elderly**
>
> The candidate in question had been included in a job for older unemployed persons. She had been unsuccessfully seeking work for 2.5 years. She was a seller and commercial technician by profession, but her last period of employment was a fixed period contract at a large retail store, which was terminated. Through the PES programme, she was employed by a company called Kostak, who offered her a contract for an indefinite period after one year.
>
> The candidate explained: "My experience of unemployment is sad, as is certainly the case for anyone who finds themself in such a situation. As a person who more difficult to employ, I was particularly happy when I learned of the programme that stimulated the employment of older persons. My new job was a challenge and a new experience. Initially, I was employed for a period of one year, but recently received an employment contract for an indefinite period of time, which made me even more motivated to work."
>
> The employer, Kostak Company, explained: "The active employment policy programme which stimulates the employment of older motivated us to employ six people. As an employer, we have always been interested in recruitment of the unemployed, because we have good experience with PES who are very responsive in providing information about appropriate candidates. Thus, we have a greater choice of candidates with the required skills and knowledge. We initially employ people for a specific time period, and then usually offer indefinite employment. We would like such programmes to be implemented also in the future because they are a benefit both to the companies as well as well as the unemployed, especially those from disadvantaged groups, who can then be re-integrated into the working population.
>
> *Source:* Interviews undertaken for LEED, 2015.

municipality, Health Care Centre Kočevje, Novo mesto Health Centre, the Roma society 'Romano Happy' and a Norwegian partner Landsforening for Pårørende innen Psykisk Helse.

The municipalities of Kočevje and Novo mesto are home to approximately 1 440 Romas. As a group, they experience poor living conditions, poor social networks, and a lack of education and unemployment. Limited access to health care is also a problem that arises because of ineffective communication with medical staff, poor recognition of symptoms and low prevention activities. A project has been set-up to address health problems in the Roma community that will offer the Roma accessible health services and prevention activities.

Adult training programmes are adapted to at-risk groups and many types of assistance exist, depending on the needs of the specific group. For example, the Peoples' university (e.g. RIC in Novo mesto) provides programmes for older and disadvantaged workers that help build general competences. They also offer project learning programmes to young drop-outs, targeting women over 40 years old and immigrants. They constantly monitor the market and data and prepare proposals to the ministry, municipality, and local PES offices in order to develop and get financing to support these programmes.

The informal sector is a significant problem in Slovenia. According to Nastav (2009), the share of informal employment is around 15% of GDP. Informal and illegal employment usually intensifies during times of crisis. The Slovenian tax administration has fought heavily against this problem, with some success. However, many workers continue to report bad practices, but the PES is able to do little other than make referrals to where these problems can be reported.

Childcare and family friendly policies to support women's participation in employment

Slovenia has a female labour force participation rate of 67.3%, compared to an OECD average of 62.8% (age 15-64). In comparing the gap between the male and female labour force participation rates in 2015, there is only a 7.5 percentage point difference in Slovenia (67.9 compared to 75.4), compared to a 16.7 percentage point difference (63.0 compared to 79.7) across the OECD (OECD, 2016a). A number of factors can influence female labour market participation, including the availability of affordable child and elderly care as well as family friendly work policies.

Availability of childcare

Slovenia also has a well-developed early childhood care system. 45% of 0 to 2 year olds and 88% of 3-5 year olds participate in childcare or school services. In both cases, this is above the OECD average (33% and 82% respectively) (OECD, 2016b). Children in Slovenia are accepted to child-care from age 11 months of age on, thus eliminating the gap between maternity leave entitlements and the legal right to care coverage. A child can spend up to 9 hours a day in childcare, allowing the parents (usually mothers) to return to their work routine. Slovenia is one of only eight EU countries that has a legal guarantee of early childhood care relatively soon after birth (beside Denmark, Germany, Estonia, Malta, Finland, Sweden and Norway). The gap between the end of compensated childcare leave and the legal entitlement to early care can be over two years in many other EU countries (Eurodyce and Eurostat, 2014).

Childcare facilities are mainly public, but many private early childcare and pre-school providers have opened in response to a recent baby boom. Generally, childcare is affordable to parents. Parents contribute to the provision of public childcare on a means-tested basis. The cost of early childcare and pre-schools in Slovenia differs across municipalities, and municipalities are able to subsidise places. In general, childcare is heavily subsidised for people with lower incomes per family member. Family circumstances (e.g. student families, etc.) can be an advantage when searching for a spot in early childcare and pre-schools.

Due to the baby-boom in recent years, the availability of public childcare has become an issue. In some regions (bigger cities), a bigger problem is that there is not enough space. For example, data from the Novo mesto (South-East Slovenia region) municipality shows that 2 more early childcare facilities or pre-schools are needed to accommodate 120 children. In Maribor, there are 36 early childcare and pre-schools (3 of which are private), and none have a significant waiting list.

To respond to the baby boom, municipalities have opened several new facilities and a significant number of private childcare facilities have also been established. The state has provided concession to some private facilities in order to ensure affordability. In addition, the state has recently acted to allow people to register as a child-caretaker and tend to up to four children at home. In the past, retired women often took care of children on an informal basis due to the lack of institutional care options available. This has helped to move unregistered or "shadow" childcare services into the formal economy.

Availability of elder care

Care for the elderly is a general problem across Slovenia, primarily related to the availability of institutionalized care (elderly homes). The ageing population has increased much faster than the number of beds in elderly homes, which has resulted in long waits for appropriate facilities. In the Drava region, there are 10 homes for the elderly and 7 in the South-East Slovenia region (including Bela Krajina and Kočevje/Ribnica). In the Maribor region (Drava), there are 2 577 people who would immediately like a free room; in Novo mesto (South-East Slovenia) there are 181. Due to long waiting periods, people sometimes submit an application many years in advance. Thus, there are over 600 people in total waiting in Novo mesto and 8 700 Maribor. While these statistics paint a grim picture, other types of support as well as informal networks alleviate the care responsibilities of younger generations. Additionally, institutionalised care is highly culturally unpopular, and thus homes often accept those with more severe problems. In general, the care-burden is low and does not inhibit employment.

However, given the ageing population in Slovenia, more could be done. New homes have been opened in the past few years and the state has also provided concessions to private suppliers to stimulate the growth of the sector. For example, the Kočevje municipality has invested in the development of modern elderly facilities that feature eco-homes with a special dementia ward, with the financial support of the Ministry of Economy and Ministry of Labour under the Programme for promotion of competitiveness of Pokolpje area. The municipality has also been certified as "friendly to elderly".

The state has also decided to intensify alternative support for elderly, particularly through help at home, which has expanded quickly since 2006. The measure is aimed at those over the age of 65 (which represent 88% of all users) who are disabled or suffer chronic illnesses. This is also very beneficial for the elderly, especially those that prefer to stay at home rather than moving to an institution. This measure is a part of social security rights and encompasses:

- Household help, including food delivery, going to the store to buy food, washing dishes, cleaning, etc. This is also the most popular service, with 84.5% of users receiving this form of help.
- Help with maintaining social contacts, including building new contacts with the help of volunteers, keeping contact with family, helping individuals make necessary trips, etc. These services are also in high demand, with 72% of users requesting this form of assistance.
- Help with everyday routine tasks, including help getting dressed, undressed, washing, help with feeding, etc. Around 60% of users need such help.

In most cases, these services are provided by social security centres and elderly homes. In 2006, 5 300 individuals were using these services, which rose to 9 664 in 2014. The number of users fluctuates significantly during the year; for example, there were 6 900 users in December 2014. Women are much more likely to use these services than men, and their share increases with age (as expected due to longer life expectancy).

Family friendly work policies

Slovenia has a relatively generous system of parental rights, especially in early childhood. A mother is entitled to 105 days of "birth" leave (30 days before the due date, the rest after birth). After the 105 days, a mother or a father can take 260 days of child-care leave. Fathers are also entitled to 20 days of paid leave, while the state pays social contributions for a further 70 days of unpaid leave. The benefit that the mother receives during her period of leave is calculated on the basis of her average income over the previous 12 months, but cannot be lower than 55% of the average Slovenian wage. The benefit for childcare leave cannot be lower than 55% of the average Slovenian wage and cannot exceed 250% of the average. One parent of young children can also opt for shorter working hours, which cannot be lower than half of normal work obligations, while the state will support social contributions for this parent on the basis of full-time work. In the case of large families, a parent can also opt to be a homemaker and the state will cover social contributions (Skupnost Centrov Za Socialno Delo, nd). Additionally, both of the regional development plans of South-East Slovenia and Drava regions stress the importance of balancing work-family life although no specific measures are provided.

Table 3.3. **Overview of parental rights**

Parental leave	Maternity leave 105 days
	Paternal leave (90 days: 20+70)
	Child-care leave (260 days)
	Adoption leave (120 or 150 days)
Benefits	Maternity benefit
	Paternity benefit
	Benefits during child-care leave
	Adoptor benefits
The right to shorter work time due to parenthood	Until child reaches age 3 years – for all children
	Until child reaches age 18 years – in case of more severe physical or mental disability
The right of parents to have their social security contributions paid in case of 4 or more children	Until the youngest child is 10 years old – due to labour market inactivity

Source: Republic of Slovenia The association of centres for social work (2017).

However, on the employer side, there is a lot of anecdotal evidence that young women face difficulties in finding work due to potential motherhood, which employers associate with frequent sick-leave. There are some large Slovenian companies are quite active in this field. Lek, a company in in Ljubljana (now Novartis), was the first to have an internal early childcare facility and pre-school. Companies that understand the need to balance work and family life can apply for a "Family-friendly company" certificate (Družini prijazno podjetje. Currently there are 240 such companies in Slovenia.

Tackling youth unemployment

The crisis significantly impacted the position of youth in the labour market – both those that just finished education as well as those that dropped out of education and are now not in education, employment or training (NEETs). In Slovenia, the share of NEETs in the 15-24 year old category is lower than in the EU28 on average. This is a result of high inclusion of youth in secondary and tertiary education.

In January 2014, the government adopted the Youth Guarantee implementation plan for the years 2014 and 2015 and subsequently developed a plan for 2016-20. The Youth Guarantee seeks to ensure that every young person aged 15 to 29 years receives an offer of employment (including traineeship), on-the-job training or enters formal education or a short form of institutional or work-based training within four months of registering with the PES. In Slovenia, this plan is being implemented through structural reforms and specific initiatives, as summarised in the table below.

Figure 3.11. **Share of Youth Not in Education, Employment or Training (NEET), age group 15-24, 2015**

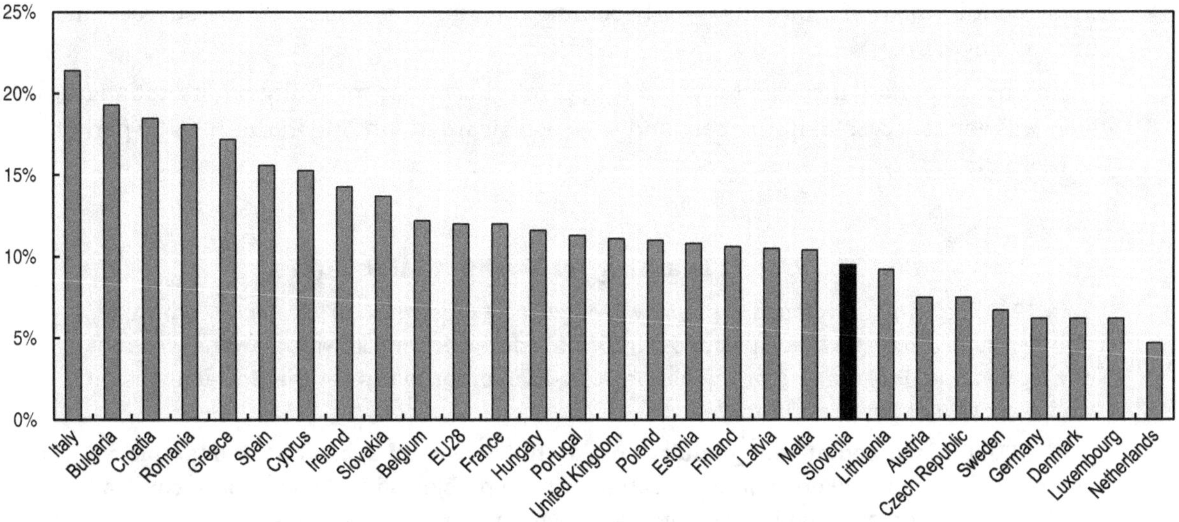

Source: Eurostat (2017b).

Table 3.4. **Overview of Youth Guarantee pathway to employment**

Preventive action	• Lifelong career guidance at all levels of education and beyond • Grants • Forecasting labour market needs • Work-based training with employers during education
Immediately after becoming unemployed	• Preparation of an individual employment plan • General and in-depth counselling and assistance in finding employment • Special youth counsellors • Active employment policy measures: project learning for young adults, formal education, preparation of national vocational qualifications, training to promote self-employment of young people, etc. • EURES
After three months of unemployment	• Repeated in-depth counselling and job-seeking assistance • Additional active employment policy measures to increase employability: on-the-job training, work-based and institutional training • Mentoring schemes • Support in the implementation of an entrepreneurial idea • Exemption from the payment of the employer's contributions (Intervention Act)
After four months of unemployment	• Additional active employment policy measures: incentives to employers to employ, co-financing of mandatory traineeship in certain sectors, etc. • Counselling service • Public works (for long-term unemployed)

Source: European Commission (2017).

As an example of the measures taken, Slovenian PES provided additional training for front line staff that work with young people, and hired additional counsellors to provide guidance and job-seeking assistance to young people. In order to create more labour market opportunities for young people, it launched the Work Trials programme in 2015 for young people up to age 29, and implemented a measure wherein employers are exempt from paying social security contributions for two years for each new young employee aged up to 30 years old (Draft Joint Employment Report from the Commission and the Council).

The first results from 2014, the first year of the implementation of the Youth Guarantee in Slovenia, are promising. In 2014, 25 742 unemployed young people found jobs, which is

23.6% more than in the previous year (2013). The latest data show that 49% of young people aged 15 to 29 years old have received a good quality offer for further training, education or employment in the first 4 months after becoming unemployed, and 32% have successfully found employment.

Another important measure for youth is the Project Learning for Young Adults initiatives, which was very successful in the past and was also awarded funding in the 2016-20 period (see Box 3.8).

> **Box 3.8. Project Learning for Young Adults: PUM-O**
>
> In 1990s Slovenia developed a publicly recognised programme of "Project Learning for Young Adults" (PUM-O) which promoted informal adult learning. The programme is part of the Operational Programme for the period 2014-20 in order to further the "Social inclusion and reduction of poverty" priority.
>
> The PUM-O is **aimed at young adults from 15 to 26 years of age**, who are unemployed or are first-time jobseekers, not in education or have problems in education that can lead to discontinuation of schooling. The programme has **two main objectives:**
>
> - Formation of professional identity, developing the candidates' sense of initiative and entrepreneurship in order to help them enter the labour market,
> - Development of learning abilities and basic skills, particularly in support of the formation of personal identity and the promotion of their active participation in society.
>
> The programme comprises **three key educational modules:**
>
> - Career planning and professional identity development includes developing both short-term and long-term career goals, preparing an employment plan and providing the basic competencies that help the individual 'behave' in the labour market (basic legislation, entrepreneurship skills, etc);
> - General education, which aims to build their general knowledge about local and global trends, society, culture, sustainable development; natural science, humanities and social sciences, promote understanding of social organisation and social relations, and improve the ability to actively use modern technologies;
> - Personal growth and sustainable lifestyle, which focuses on interpersonal relationships and group-dynamic processes, physical and mental health, sexuality, etiquette, cuisine, culture of living, planning and leisure activities, entertainment, consumption and abuse of alcohol and other drugs, crime and violence in the family, among peers and in other social situations.
>
> In the beginning, the candidate and mentor prepare a personal career plan that defines the purpose of the candidate's participation (vision) and targets (including time goals). Implementation is periodically monitored and, also changed when needed. The participant and mentors also work with other institutions and third parties (e.g. employment advisors at PES, school counsellors, mentors in enterprises, or parents).
>
> PUM-O is one year long and includes the individual in activities from Monday to Friday for six hours a day. The duration can be reduced or increased, depending on the needs of the career plan and external circumstances. The participants obtain a certificate that provides data on the individual's participation, his/her individual learning projects and other achievements and activities.
>
> Source: Translation and adaptation from Slovenian Institute for Adult Education (2015).

Openness to immigration

In comparison to other OECD countries, Slovenia does not receive a large number of immigrants. According to SORS (2015) data, approximately 14 000 immigrants arrived in 2014, representing 0.6% of the population. The immigrants are primarily men (60-80% of all immigrants) aged between 20 and 49 years of age who come in search of work. Traditionally, the majority of immigrants to Slovenia come from Bosnia and Herzegovina, Croatia, the Former Yugoslav Republic of Macedonia, Kosovo, Montenegro, and Serbia (around two-thirds of all migrants). Generally, these migrants speak Serbo-Croatian (except for younger people from Kosovo), which facilitates their integration, as this language is spoken by or understood by the majority of Slovenians.

Figure 3.12. **Immigration to Slovenia: number of immigrants, 1990-2015**

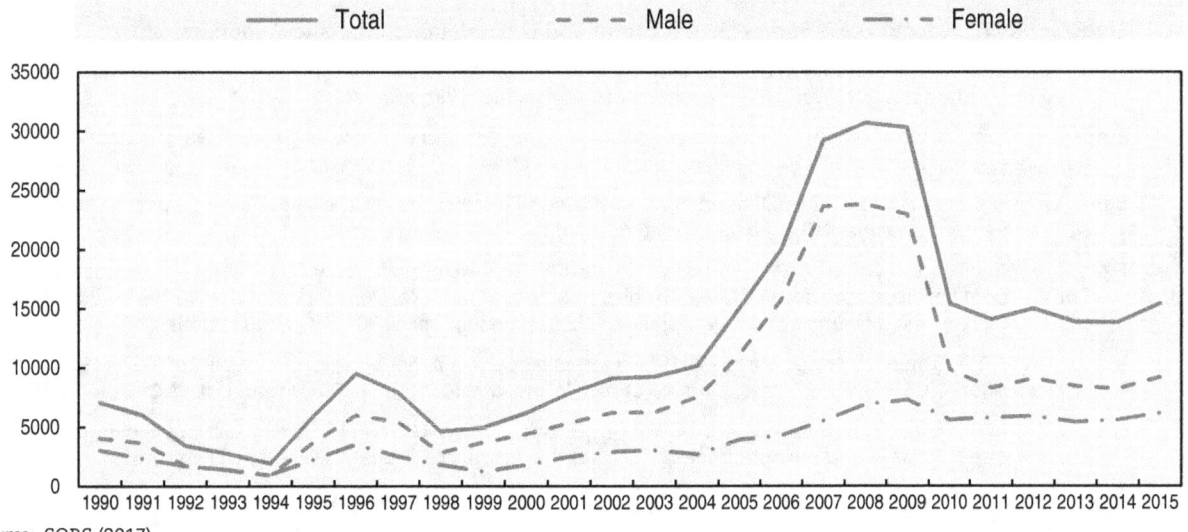

Source: SORS (2017).

In the past, PES supported the integration of immigrants through an informational "one-stop-shop". However, the office ceased operations from 30 September 2015. Foreign workers are now able to obtain information at PES and municipalities, as well as other institutions such as peoples' university and the not-for-profit sector. Programmes to ease integration are available (Slovenian language courses as well as "preliminary integration courses").

Work permits legislation has been simplified to ensure that foreigners from non-EU countries no longer need two separate permits (one to work and one to live in Slovenia). Foreigners seeking to enter Slovenia and find employment are now able to apply for a single permit at the local municipality.

Immigrants must submit their education certificates through a formal notification procedure in order to have foreign formal education qualifications recognised. Vocational competences can be recognized (validated) for a number of vocational qualifications by obtaining a national vocational qualification certificate in accordance with National Professional Qualifications Act. Some qualifications can be transferred (for example, those from the EU). ENIC-NARIC Centre Slovenia provides information regarding the comparability of specific elements of immigrants' education with the Slovenian education system.

References

Center Grm (2015), "Nagovor direktorja", [Address by the director], *www.grm-nm.si/predstavitev/nagovor-direktorja*.

CPI (2015), "Značilnosti izobraževalnih programov", [Characteristics of educational programs], *www.cpi.si/kurikul/podlage-za-pripravo-izobrazevalnih/znacilnosti-izobrazevalnih-programov.aspx*.

CPI (2014), Priprava projekta « Nacionalni organi za vajeništvo », [Preparation of the project « National organs for apprenticeship »], *www.skupnost-vss.si/wp-content/uploads/2014/06/Vajenistvo_razpis_26junij2014.pdf*.

EU Barometer (2010), "Employers perception of graduate employability: Analytical report", *Flash Eurobarometer 304*, http://ec.europa.eu/commfrontoffice/publicopinion/flash/fl_304_en.pdf.

Employment Service of the Republic of Slovenia (2015), "Napovednik zaposlovanja", [Forecasting employment], published with permission of PES.

European Commission (2017), "Youth Guarantee country by country: Slovenia", *www.ec.europa.eu/social/BlobServlet?docId=13660&langId=en*.

Eurostat (2017a), Labour Force Survey "Employment and Labour Market Statistics", (database).

Eurostat (2017b), "Young people neither in employment nor in education and training by sex and NUTS 2 regions", (dataset), http://ec.europa.eu/eurostat/web/products-datasets/-/edat_lfse_22.

Eurostat (2016), Eurostat on-line "LFS series – detailed quarterly survey results (from 1998 onwards)", database, http://ec.europa.eu/eurostat/en/web/products-datasets/-/LFSQ_URGAED.

Eurodyce and Eurostat (2014), "Key Data on Early Childhood Education and Care", http://eacea.ec.europa.eu/education/eurydice/documents/key_data_series/166EN.pdf.

Froy, F., S. Giguère, L. Pyne and D.E. Wood (2011), "Building Flexibility and Accountability Into Local Employment Services: Synthesis of OECD Studies in Belgium, Canada, Denmark and the Netherlands", *OECD Local Economic and Employment Development (LEED) Working Papers*, 2011/10, OECD Publishing.

Manpower (2015), "Talent Shortage Survey 2015", *www.manpowergroup.com/wps/wcm/connect/408f7067-ba9c-4c98-b0ec-dca74403a802/2015_Talent_Shortage_Survey-lo_res.pdf?MOD=AJPERES&ContentCache=NONE*.

Nastav, B. (2009), "Siva ekonomija v Sloveniji: Merjenje, vzroki in posledice", [Gray economy in Slovenia: Measurement, causes and consequences], doctoral dissertation. Ljubljana: Faculty of Economics.

OECD (forthcoming, 2017a), *OECD Skills Strategy diagnostic report: Slovenia*, OECD Publishing, Paris.

OECD (forthcoming, 2017b), *OECD Economic Surveys: Slovenia 2017*, OECD Publishing, Paris.

OECD (2017c), "Labour market programmes: Expenditure and participants", *OECD Employment and Labour Market Statistics* (database), http://dx.doi.org/10.1787/data-00312-en, (accessed on 27 June 2017).

OECD (2016a), Labour force participation rate (indicator), http://dx.doi.org/10.1787/8a801325-en, (accessed on 2 August 2016).

OECD (2016b), "Family Indicators", *OECD Social and Welfare Statistics* (database), http://dx.doi.org/10.1787/efd30a09-en, (accessed on 02 August 2016).

OECD (2016c), *Connecting People with Jobs: The Labour Market, Activation Policies and Disadvantaged Workers in Slovenia*, OECD Publishing, Paris, http://dx.doi.org/10.1787/9789264265349-en.

OECD (2016d), *OECD Employment Outlook 2016*, OECD Publishing, Paris, http://dx.doi.org/10.1787/empl_outlook-2016-en.

OECD (2016e), *Job Creation and Local Economic Development 2016*, OECD Publishing, Paris, http://dx.doi.org/10.1787/9789264261976-en.

OECD (2015a), "How does Slovenia compare?", country note to the *OECD Employment Outlook*, 2015, *www.oecd.org/slovenia/Employment-Outlook-Slovenia-EN.pdf*.

OECD (2015b), *OECD Science, Technology and Industry Scoreboard 2015: Innovation for growth and society*, OECD Publishing, Paris, http://dx.doi.org/10.1787/sti_scoreboard-2015-en.

OECD (2015c), *OECD Economic Surveys: Slovenia 2015*, OECD Publishing, Paris, http://dx.doi.org/10.1787/eco_surveys-svn-2015-en.

OECD (2014), *Job Creation and Local Economic Development*, OECD Publishing, Paris, http://dx.doi.org/10.1787/9789264215009-en.

Pahor, M. et al. (2012), Analiza povpraševanja po delu v Sloveniji v okviru modela strateškega prestrukturiranja podjetij: Zaključno poročilo. Ljubljana: Ekonomska fakulteta Univerze v Ljubljani, Koper: Fakulteta za management Univerze na Primorskem.

Regionalni razvojni program za podravsko razvojno regijo [Regional development plan Drava region] (2015), *www.mra.si/wp-content/uploads/2015/01/RRP-PODRAVJE-2014-20202.pdf*.

Regionalni razvojni program za obdobje 2014-2020 v razvojni regiji Jugovzhodna Slovenija (Regional development plan for the Soth-East Slovenia region) (2015), *www.rc-nm.si/Portals/0/RRP%202014-2020%20oddan/RRP_JVSLO_2014-2020_marec%202015.pdf*.

Republic of Slovenia Government Office for Development and European Cohesion Policy (2017), "Subsidy for self-employment", *www.eu-skladi.si/kohezija-do-2013/funds/best-practices/op-ropi/subsidy-for-self-employment* (accessed 23 June 2017).

Republic of Slovenia The association of centres for social work (2017), "Parental Protection", *www.scsd.si/parental-protection.html* (accessed 23 June 2017).

RIC (Razvojno izobraževalni center Novo mesto) (2015), Homepage, *www.ric-nm.si/si/*.

Slovenian Institute for Adult Education (2015), "Projektno učenje mlajših odraslih", [Project Learning for Young Adults], *www.acs.si/pum*.

SORS (Statistical office of the Republic of Slovenia) (2017), SI-STAT "Data by Statistical Regions", (SORS on-line database), *http://pxweb.stat.si/pxweb/Database/Regions/Regions.asp*, Svet regije JV Slovenije (Council for SE Slovenia region) 2015, *www.rc-nm.si/Regionalnirazvoj/SvetregijeJVSlovenije.aspx*.

SORS (Statistical office of the Republic of Slovenia) (2015), Med delovno aktivnimi osebami je bilo v letu 2014 več kot polovica medobčinskih delovnih migrantov, *www.stat.si/StatWeb/prikazi-novico?id=5160&idp=3&headerbar=2*.

Zakon o poklicnem in strokovnem izobraževanju (ZPSI-1) [Vocational and Professional Education Act] (2006), Uradni list RS, 79/2006, *http://pisrs.si/Pis.web/pregledPredpisa?id=ZAKO4325*.

ZLUS (2015), "Članice Zveze ljudskih univerz Slovenije" [Members of the Association of Human Universities of Slovenia], *http://zlus.si/si/clanice_zlus.aspx*.

Chapter 4

Towards an action plan for jobs in Slovenia: Recommendations and best practices

Stimulating job creation at the local level requires integrated action across the employment, training, and economic development portfolios. Co-ordinated place-based policies can help workers find suitable jobs, while also contributing to demand by stimulating productivity. This requires flexible policy management frameworks, information, and integrated partnerships which leverage the efforts of local stakeholders. This chapter outlines the key recommendations that have emerged from the OECD Review of Local Job Creation in Slovenia.

Better aligning programmes and policies to local economic development

Recommendation: Inject flexibility into the management of employment programmes and policies at the local level

In Slovenia, programmes are designed nationally and provide limited strategic flexibility for local employment offices to tailor programming to local labour markets. Local and regional offices can provide input during the preparation stage of the development of programmes and policies, but their overall influence is low. This limited input from local offices can have a negative impact on overall implementation. It is recommended that the public employment service provide some degree of flexibility to regional and local offices in the management of employment policies. OECD research has articulated the benefits for providing flexibility within programme design and eligibility criteria, outsourcing arrangements, budget management, and strategic approach.

It is important to differentiate between operational and strategic flexibility. Operational flexibility applies to the delivery of programmes, and refers to the leeway given to individual case officers to decide on the type of policy intervention that should be used to serve an unemployed client. In an operationally flexible system, service providers would, for example, be able to determine which available services should be provided to a particular client ranging from facilitated self-service to different types of training and/or intensive counselling. Strategic flexibility applies when the local employment service takes a leadership role in adjusting programmes and policies to their local labour market.

The government could examine the possibility of providing some budget flexibility to local offices to design and implement their own programmes and strategies for employment and job creation. Special conditions could be placed on this flexible budget envelope to ensure that local PES offices use this funding to foster partnerships and collaboration with other local stakeholders when delivering programmes. This type of mechanism would provide local PES offices with some latitude to fit programmes to local labour market needs, which are different across Slovenia and would be welcomed by local PES offices. Box 4.1 describes examples of how OECD countries inject flexibility into the budget management of public employment services.

In determining whether or not to award flexibility at the local level, the government should examine the capacity of regional and local offices to ensure they are sufficient to manage this responsibility. Providing flexibility at the local level can lead to unintended consequences and inequitable service provision if it is not provided incrementally and where strong capacities exist.

Recommendation: Create a co-ordinated action plan for jobs and simplify institutional arrangements and responsibilities across the range of government actors

There is a dense network of actors in Slovenia who have a role to play in designing and delivering employment, skills, and economic development policies. This demonstrates the importance placed on developing and utilising a skilled workforce for better economic

> **Box 4.1. How do OECD countries inject flexibility into the budget management of public employment services?**
>
> **Quebec, Canada:** In Quebec, Canada, local employment centres are provided with considerable autonomy from the provincial level in determining how to target employment and training programmes to local client groups within a flexible funding pool allocated from the regional employment office.
>
> **Czech Republic:** Regional offices can move over 15% of their budget line with prior approval from the Directorate General of the Labour Office.
>
> **Flanders, Belgium:** VDAB (the public employment services agency) in Flanders, Belgium has also moved towards a more flexible employment services model. A board of provincial directors takes decisions autonomously, developing provincial business plans within the framework of the plan for the whole Flanders region. With regard to budget management, local employment offices have the ability to devote about 20% of their budget envelope to locally-designed strategies. This means that local VDAB representatives are able to take a stronger leadership role locally, with the local representative in the city of Antwerp galvanising actors to work together to tackle employment issues in particular local sectors.
>
> Source: OECD (2014a), *Job Creation and Local Economic Development*, OECD Publishing, Paris.

development opportunities. However, there are a number of challenges associated with the current structure. For one, parallel strategies are being prepared at the national and regional level at the same time by different actors, which can create duplication and inefficiencies in policy implementation. At the national level, awareness of the initiatives and policies of other ministries is weak, which can lead to fragmentation and inefficient service delivery at the local level. Likewise, at the local level, communication and co-ordination between the various stakeholders was reported to be insufficient. Overall, there is an opportunity to simplify institutional arrangements to improve overall performance with the public sector while enabling stronger co-operation and integration on the ground. A clearer division of responsibilities would allow for more efficient co-operation.

A gap that emerged during this OECD review was a lack of a co-ordinating structure to bring together public employment services, education and training institutions, economic development actors and employers in a structured way at the local level. In order to address this, the government should examine the possibility of piloting the establishment of a local board in one or two regions. Such boards could be tasked with co-ordinating the relevant policy portfolios and provided with a funding envelope to introduce joint programmes under a regional employment and economic development strategy, potentially linked with the national action plan for jobs. A small budget that would be distributed regionally could help to stimulate co-operation at regional/local level.

This would give local communities more opportunity to frame and manage the policies that are implemented in their area. With the goal of simplifying institutional structures, it would be important to identify a local lead organisation/actor. This would be a core regional institution that would have the responsibility for regularly working with important regional and local stakeholders to actively manage regional/local development. Such a leader should be empowered with both adequate human and financial resources. For example of how this has been in done in New York City, see Box 4.2.

There are a number of institutions that could play this role, including the Regional Development Agencies, regional public employment service offices, Adult Education

> **Box 4.2. Career Pathways: One City Working Together, New York City**
>
> While New York City accounts for a large proportion of the Untied State's GDP, it also faces significant challenges related to growing income inequality. Like many other places, job growth in recent years has been concentrated in high-wage/high skill and low-wage/low-skill industries, and the rising number of working poor face limited career progression opportunities. At the same time, employers report facing a shortage of high-skilled workers. Despite the fact that New York City's workforce development system has a budget of approximately USD 500 million a year, serving roughly 500 000 clients, it was not well suited to address these challenges. The city's workforce system spanned multiple agencies, with each agency having its own set of goals, rules and processes. In addition, unions, private employers, philanthropy and non-profits also provided workforce programmes and training.
>
> In 2014, the mayor convened the Jobs for New Yorkers Task Force to set new priorities for employment and training programmes across agencies. This task force was overseen by the Mayor's Office of Workforce Development and brought together actors from the "supply" side of the workforce (educators, non-profit leaders, advocates, union leaders, and philanthropists) and the "demand" side (business leaders and employers). It identified a need to re-orient the system away from simple job placement to career development and need to better align programmes and services across agencies, including creating stronger linkages with the city's economic development activities. More concretely, it identified the following priorities:
>
> - **Building Skills Employers Seek:** focus on connecting New Yorkers to quality jobs with family-supporting wages and career advancement potential, including creating strong Industry Partnerships that provide robust feedback loops with companies in priority sectors of New York's economy.
> - **Improving Job Quality:** reward worker-friendly business practices such as consistent scheduling, access to commuter benefits and financial empowerment services.
> - **Increasing System and Policy Co-ordination:** align workforce and economic development initiatives, utilizing local legislation and administrative policies as key levers to promote career pathway development and implementation.
>
> These priorities have been operationalized into 10 recommendations, with progress being tracked on each. More information is available at *www1.nyc.gov/site/careerpathways/index.page*.
>
> Source: The City of New York (2014), "Career Pathways: One City Working Together", *www1.nyc.gov/assets/careerpathways/downloads/pdf/career-pathways-full-report.pdf*; The City of New York (2015), "Career Pathways: Progress Update", *www1.nyc.gov/assets/careerpathways/downloads/pdf/Career-Pathways-Progress-Update.pdf*.

Advisory Boards, and local public authorities. However, in many places, some combination of lack of capacity, lack of leadership skills, lack of community trust, or lack of statutory power hinders their ability to effectively adopt this responsibility.

During the course of this OECD review, discussions revealed that local PES offices have strong credibility and trust and therefore could potentially play such an intermediary and anchor role. Regional development agencies are an important actor in this space but many local organisations appear less than satisfied with the current level of engagement and dialogue that is undertaken. To more broadly fulfil these responsibilities, more efforts are needed from the regional development agencies to reach out and work with local partners and stakeholders to define strategic objectives from a regional development perspective.

Recommendation: Use local labour market information and intelligence to conduct more evaluations on the strengths and weaknesses of EU-funded projects

There are a broad range of programmes available to assist and activate the unemployed back into the labour market. However, in many cases, the nature of project financing for many employment and economic development programmes hinders their sustainability. The government should examine opportunities for working more closely with regional and local employment and economic development organisations to better plan for the sustainability of programmes and determine which could be financed over a longer-term basis.

In addition to examining how to provide more sustainable funding for successful programmes, the government should seek to strengthen the overall evaluation culture of active labour market programmes to inform future planning and development. Programme and policy evaluations can provide insights into which policies are most effective and/or how programmes should be reformed to make them efficient. A stronger evaluation approach in Slovenia would enable policy-makers to choose appropriate measures and stimulate the rational use of resources available.

An important component of using a more evidence-based approach is having access to good data and information. It is necessary to have strong reliable data that are recent and interpreted within the right labour market context. In Slovenia, there is a strong level of data available on labour market trends which enable trend analysis within regions. More work could be done on skills forecasting and anticipating future demand. Local universities and research centres could play a stronger role in this area where capacity exists. The government should examine opportunities within the Ministry of Labour to undertake more analysis on the future needs of the economy. An international example of this approach is detailed in Box 4.3.

Box 4.3. Ireland Expert Group on Future Skills Needs

The main Irish state agency for data analysis is the Expert Group on Future Skills Needs (EGFSN) which advises the Irish government on current and future skills needs of the economy and on other labour market issues that impact Ireland's enterprise and employment growth. Established in 1997, the EGFSN reports to the Minister for Jobs, Enterprise and Innovation and the Minister for Education and Skills and is funded by the National Training Fund. Forfás provides it with research and secretariat support while the FÁS Skills and Labour Market Research Unit (SLMRU) provides it with data, analysis and research and manages the National Skills Database.

There are a number of main sources for regional and local data collection and analysis. An annual National Skills Bulletin provides estimates of skills shortages across the full range of Standard Occupational Classifications, carried out by the EGFSN. This contains a short section on regional skills profiles but does not provide the same level of detail, and sector-specific analyses are likely to be ad hoc. In 2012, the EGFSN also published regional labour market profiles which have significant potential to support regional decision making by education and training providers, as well as career guidance and immigration services. These profiles extract data from the Central Statistics Office, government departments, the state development agencies and other sources to sketch the characteristics of each region's economic structure and workforce. The data and analysis comes from the SLMRU and its National Skills Database.

Source: OECD (2014b), *Employment and Skills Strategies in Ireland*, OECD Reviews on Local Job Creation, OECD Publishing, Paris, http://dx.doi.org/10.1787/9789264207912-en.

Adding value through skills

Recommendation: Create a well-functioning apprenticeship system that better connects training opportunities to the workplace

The importance of developing a well-functioning and effective apprenticeship system has gained traction within many OECD countries following the global financial crisis, as countries seek to reduce youth unemployment and better link education and skills policies to the workplace. Apprenticeships and other work-based training opportunities provide an effective mechanism to build stronger connections between training providers and employers, while ensuring that individuals receive a good mix of theoretical and practical skills. Slovenia lacks a well-functioning apprenticeship system. There is currently a national working group on reforming apprenticeships, but key sticking points include the status of apprentices (whether pupils or employees), how costs will be shared between the government and employers, how to ensure quality, especially in SMEs, and concerns that taking on apprentices will actually reduce productivity in SMEs.

During the course of this OECD study, stakeholders were unclear about the current state of apprenticeship opportunities in Slovenia. Therefore, it is important that the government develops a communication strategy going forward about what apprenticeship opportunities exist as well as the benefits to be obtained from participating. During discussions undertaken for this review, employers were critical of the knowledge and skills of recent training graduates. Many employers in Slovenia would welcome an expansion of apprenticeship opportunities.

At the local level, municipalities could play a stronger role in working with local employers to demonstrate the benefits of participating in the apprenticeship system. This could include setting up information session, breakfast meetings, or city councils to actively encourage employers to participate in any new apprenticeship programmes. For example, in the UK, local apprenticeship hubs have been set up in the city of Manchester and the Leeds City Region to act as central co-ordinating and marketing organisations to engage with employers and individuals on apprenticeship programmes.

Local leadership from key stakeholders is particularly important in ensuring the effective implementation of apprenticeship systems. For example, in the New Zealand town of Otorohanga, employers and young people were targeted by a group of concerned local leaders, including the mayor, church leaders and major employers. The activism and leadership from these actors resulted in custom initiatives to improve apprenticeship participation and completion rates, including personalised assistance, increasing access to off-the-job vocational training and personal pastoral care. The mayor, a former apprentice himself, prioritised the development of a network of local stakeholders to improve the outcomes of the apprenticeship system and to reach out to local employers. Designing an effective apprenticeship system will be a challenge in Slovenia as there is an obligation to build stronger employer buy-in as well as capacity within the vocational education and training system. In trying to develop more apprenticeship opportunities, the government should also ensure that quality apprenticeships are available in new and emerging occupations. This would include looking at how to expand apprenticeship opportunities beyond the traditional manufacturing and construction sectors.

> Box 4.4. **Key Policy Principles from the German Apprenticeship Model**
>
> **A more transparent, simpler transition for young people**
>
> - Make the apprenticeship route an attractive option for good school performers but also ensure entry mechanisms for weaker school performers;
> - Ensure schools have good links with firms and further training and tertiary education institutions, alongside strong career guidance;
> - Pre-apprenticeship courses can serve as means to better prepare young people for a vocational route and to integrate more young people from disadvantaged backgrounds into apprenticeships;
> - Training contracts can be offered to each school leaver with the necessary general skills and who is seeking an apprenticeship. Those not offered an in-company apprenticeship should be offered a recognised alternative by an external provider.
>
> **Improving work organisation**
>
> - Ensure good work organisation in firms. This includes having high numbers of skilled workers and recruiting managers from the shop floor, thereby ensuring they have the technical skills and good insight into the company. This in turn can promote access to training and results in a mix of management types;
> - More decentralised forms of work organisation and giving workers more autonomy can bring about better quality work and allow apprentices to more fully utilise their skills, thus resulting in productivity increases.
>
> **Access to career advancement training**
>
> - Supplement initial vocational training with advancement training to enable apprentices to progress to higher level jobs. In addition to specific occupational courses, general components could be included in this training, such as business administration and apprenticeship pedagogy;
> - It is critical that advancement courses are certified and fit into national qualification frameworks so that apprentices who complete them can widen their professional prospects and are more mobile in the internal and external labour market.
>
> **Broad apprenticeship occupations**
>
> - Broader apprenticeship occupations mean more mobility and flexibility for apprentices. They also ensure more transferable skills, meaning workers are less vulnerable to unemployment in the face of an economic slowdown;
> - Provide a mix of training for apprentices in joint core competences (such as teamwork) and occupation-specific competences. Commitment to providing training and safeguarding apprenticeships
> - An effective apprenticeship system is dependent on employers being committed to providing training. Agreements between the key social partners at all government levels can be crucial in re-engaging employers, particularly as more seek to reduce training costs following the economic crisis;
> - Training pacts at the national, regional and local level can be a good way to ensure involvement by social partners and strong employer representation (e.g. via employers' associations, chambers of commerce, as well as unions and government). These do not necessarily require additional financing;
> - Put in place mechanisms to keep apprentices on in times of high unemployment and to provide employment after completion, if even for a limited duration.
>
> Source: Evans, S. and G. Bosch (2012), "Apprenticeships in London: Boosting Skills in a City Economy – With Comment on Lessons from Germany", OECD Local Economic and Employment Development (LEED) Working Papers, No. 2012/08, OECD Publishing, Paris, http://dx.doi.org/10.1787/5k9b9mjcxp35-en.

Recommendation: Encourage participation in adult education by developing upskilling and retraining opportunities

Developing efficient life-long learning systems that provide opportunities for upskilling and retraining throughout people's careers is becoming increasingly important as technological and structural transformations reshape labour market demands and requirements (OECD, 2016a). At present, the education and training system in Slovenia has a strong youth focus and does not provide sufficient life-long learning opportunities. While young people are encouraged to pursue tertiary education through free tuition and scholarships schemes, older workers and part-time students are generally not entitled to such financial support. As a result, participation in formal or informal training is particularly low among disadvantaged population groups, such as the low skilled. The lack of incentives for older workers to upgrade and renew their skills has led to a major generational skills gap and explains for a large part the low employment rate among older population groups.

A number of steps could be taken to reform the Slovenian life-long learning system so as to allow more workers to progress in their career, adapt to new occupational standards, or change occupation as the structure of the economy evolves. First, financial support for pursuing higher education and training programmes could be extended to older worker as well as part-time students. A training voucher system could be put in place, with priority given to job seekers with low skills levels as well as workers whose jobs are at risk of being displaced.

The way training programmes for adult are designed is also crucial. Training providers should be encouraged to offer a range of training that is tailored to the specific needs of potential target groups. For example, online and distance learning may be more adapted to those in employment or those living outside of major urban centres. Box 4.4 shows an example of such approach in Ireland. Introducing flexibility in the design of training courses, by developing part-time and modular courses, may also contribute to making training offers more attractive to a larger audience.

Box 4.4. FÁS E-College in Ireland: Flexible responses to the skill needs of learners

Online courses in the E-College, set up by FÁS, are designed to be a flexible response to the specific skill needs of job ready individuals who require training with certification to assist them to re-enter the labour market. Online courses are available free of charge to unemployed clients. Courses are also available, for a fee, to employed persons who wish to update their skills. These courses are delivered completely online and technical support is also provided. All FÁS online courses last for 14 weeks, but learners continue to have access to the course and materials for a further ten weeks (i.e. 24 weeks in total). Over 30 courses are available and course categories include Operating Systems, Networking and Technical Support, Software Development/Programming, Office Applications, Web Design/Multimedia, and Soft Skills. Learners are able to participate in blended learning courses in selected areas in the near future, which provide additional online tutor support and a range of online training with enhanced learner supports including telephone, email, E-tutor and instructor led workshops. Some courses may also include one to one, group mentoring, assignments or project work.

Source: OECD (2014b), *Employment and Skills Strategies in Ireland*, OECD Reviews on Local Job Creation, OECD Publishing, Paris, http://dx.doi.org/10.1787/9789264207912-en.

Public Employment Services have a key role to play in driving such changes. They should encourage more people to participate in upskilling and retraining activities, seek to activate jobseekers as early as possible, and focus their efforts on those workers that are the most difficult to place.

Recommendation: Strengthen local employer ownership in the design and delivery of skills development opportunities

Overall, there is a wide variety of training available. Up to 20% of the nationally set VET curriculum is "open" to enable tailoring at the local level, which creates a space for engaging local employers. However, during this OECD review, local stakeholders reported that this allows the tweaking of existing programmes while there is a stronger need to enable flexibility in overall programme delivery. Capacity also poses a challenge in some places, especially in more remote areas where the economies of scale necessary to deliver some VET programmes are not available. Poland has recently adopted a regional approach to VET to help overcome similar challenges.

> **Box 4.5. Taking a regional approach to VET in Poland**
>
> In the Dolnośląski Region of Poland, the regional authorities diagnosed a number of deficiencies in vocational education. On this basis, they planned a regional programme of vocational education development, including the selection of seven economic sectors of special importance for the regional labour market, and then set up vocational training centres related to these sectors in 9 counties. The distribution of the centres was spread evenly throughout the region. The Programme included investments in infrastructure (modern equipment for vocational education), as well as investments in the competences of teachers and students (additional lessons for students, intensive co-operation with local employers, educational and vocational counselling for students).
>
> This programme is a good example of the co-ordination of VET development in a region, which requires establishing a good partnership among regional and local authorities, implementation in a planned and systematic manner, and taking a selective approach to improving the quality of vocational education. It is also an example of good co-ordination between different instruments: investments in the infrastructure were finance by the European Regional Development Fund (ERDF), while investments in competences were finance by the European Social Fund (ESF).
>
> Source: OECD (2016b), *Employment and Skills Strategies in Poland*, OECD Publishing, Paris.

This OECD review has highlighted a number of comprehensive efforts that are being made by employers in the Drava and South-East Slovenia regions to provide skills upgrade opportunities. Furthermore, inter-company training centres (MIC) are an interesting example of successful collaboration between the VET system and local companies. The government needs to build on these efforts to identify local companies who can take a leadership role in reaching out to other employers to promote the benefits of VET and advise training institutions on curriculum development and delivery.

OECD research has shown that one way of addressing potential skills shortages and mismatch is by ensuring that employers are fully involved in the employment and training system. This means providing employers with a forum to advice on their training needs, while also having them take a lead role in the delivery of training opportunities to develop a skilled workforce. In trying to better align the supply of skills and educational opportunities to local job opportunities; it is necessary to strengthen the overall engagement of employers. This includes using employers in an advisory capacity as well as in the overall delivery of certain programmes and policies. The quality of training opportunities could be improved by providing strong incentives to employers to collaborate with the training system.

In the UK, Employer Ownership pilots have been introduced giving employers direct access to government subsidies for workforce training as opposed to the traditional arrangement whereby all government funding goes direct to colleges and training providers (OECD, 2014a), while an example of employer leadership in Australia can also provide inspiration (see Box 4.6).

> **Box 4.6. Employer leadership to attract and retain apprentices in Australia**
>
> The ABN Group in **Australia** consists of 23 companies that supply a range of services to the residential and commercial construction markets, from financing to property development, and from building to renovations. One of its companies, ABN Training, is the Group's own specialised training arm that was specifically established to manage the apprenticeship programme operating across the ABN Group of companies.
>
> The ABN Group employs 1 700 people, and engages more than 3 000 construction contractors. Around 20% of their workforce is currently comprised of apprentices, compared to an average of approximately 5% amongst the construction sector as a whole in Western Australia.
>
> The main goal of ABN Training's apprenticeship programme is to achieve the highest possible retention of graduated apprentices within the ABN Group, with the broad aim of guaranteeing future accessibility to tradespeople that are skilled to ABN Group's standards and organisational culture. Underlining this is the aim of being able to achieve generational change in standards relative to core issues such as safety, work readiness and quality of work.
>
> The ABN Group is involved in a number of corporate social responsibility and community initiatives through the ABN Foundation, its not-for-profit foundation. ABN Training, besides implementing the company's workforce development strategy, is also seen as an adjunct to the Group's commitment to corporate social responsibility, incorporating its owners' desire to improve lives through access to high quality training and contributing to up-skilling the construction sector as a whole.
>
> The ABN Group's workforce development strategy has a "whole of life" approach, and consists of three phases:
>
> - Promotion of career paths in the construction industry to Year 10-12 students;
> - In-house delivered apprenticeship programme; and
> - A "graduation" programme offering employment solutions both within the ABN Group and the broader building and construction industry to maximise the retention of graduated apprentices.
>
> The main innovation implemented by ABN Group's apprenticeship model has been adapting the standard Group Training Organisation (GTO) arrangement into an internal, enterprise-embedded structure. By doing this, the company has been able to take ownership of its apprenticeship programme as a key part of its workforce development strategy and train apprentices in a way that is aligned with its brand and organisational culture.
>
> Source: OECD/ILO (2017).

Targeting policy to local employment sectors and investing in quality jobs

Recommendation: Focus efforts on the better utilisation of skills to stimulate innovation and productivity

In Slovenia, the development and launch of the Smart Specialisation Strategy will guide EU investments going forward. The strategy aims to improve the overall position of the Slovenian economy and increase exports through the better use and development of technology. With the goal of creating innovative and productive local companies, there is an opportunity to start focusing government policies on the better utilisation of skills.

Investment in the supply of skills alone will not be sufficient to secure job creation and productivity in all local economies. The degree to which local employers are demanding and using skills also has to be taken into account. Low demand for skills amongst employers and poor utilisation of skills can undermine productivity. It can also reduce the quality of local jobs in terms of salaries, job security and the possibility for career progression. A situation of low skills trap can develop where there is a concentration of employers in a region that are pursuing price-based competition strategies that rely on low-skilled and standardised production or services. This is often a problem experienced by more peripheral rural regions. Such regions can fall into a vicious circle as it does not pay for people to invest in skills when skills are not valued by employers.

Skills utilisation policies complement supply side solutions by focusing on working with employers to improve how they use the skills of the employees in the workplace, either by re-organising work practices or by moving to more skill-intensive and higher value-added products and services. This review has examined the extent to which 1) the public sector works with employers to improve skills utilisation and work organisation; 2) sector/industry bodies are involved in such activities; and 3) universities and training institutions undertake applied research of relevance to the local economy. Of the above three areas, it was most common for universities and training institutions to be undertaking applied research of relevance to the local economy to Slovenia. This suggests that public agencies could do more to promote the better utilisation of skills within local sectors of importance.

On a case-by-case approach, the government could examine opportunities to provide regional and sectoral support to specific local employers to assist them in upgrading their production process or re-organise work (see Box 4.7 for examples of how this has been done in other places). Employment agencies can also play an important role in helping firms to better utilise their workforce, for example by supporting the development of career progression opportunities for lower-skilled workers. VET and other education institutions can also play a larger role in working with employers to upgrade production processes or conducting applied research. If established, local boards could also be tasked with looking at these more entrenched skills issues that fall outside of any single policy domain, which would complement efforts that have been launched through the Smart Specialisation Strategy (see Box 4.7).

Box 4.7. **Examples of approaches to fostering skills utilisation**

Liideri in Finland. Tekes (the Finnish Funding Agency for Technology and Innovation), runs a number of programmes to foster innovation, including "Liideri – Business, Productivity and Joy at Work Programme". Unlike more traditional innovation programmes, this programme focuses workplace development, in particular developing management practices and forms of working that promote the active utilisation of the

> Box 4.7. **Examples of approaches to fostering skills utilisation** (cont.)
>
> skills and competences of employees. Liideri is the latest in a series of publicly funded workplace innovation programmes in Finland, which were first launched in 1993. While these programmes were initially co-ordinated through the Ministry of Labour, in 2008 there were transferred to Tekes. This transfer was part of the adoption of a new national innovation strategy that emphasises demand and user-driven innovation and non-technological innovations.
>
> The Liideri project has three focus areas: renewal of management; employee participation in renewal of products, services and their production; and new forms of work organisation and working. A number of instruments are used to effect change in these areas, including work organisation development projects, integrated R&D projects, funding for research, and widespread dissemination of the outcomes
>
> **Innovative Workplaces in the UK.** The Innovative Workplaces programme was a regional pilot initiative in 2009-10, funded by the East Midlands Development Agency. It was intended that the project would benefit a small cohort of business leaders, managers and supervisors across ten organisations, each of which would benefit from long-term organisational change. The project was justified as a means of breaking out of the low skills trap by developing and unleashing the enterprise skills and competencies of those in work, enabling employees to use their initiative to innovate and create new business strategies and solutions whilst achieving maximum productivity. Both UK WON, a not-for-profit body involved in disseminating and developing innovative workplace practice, and Acas, a UK government body with a tripartite structure, charged with promoting and facilitating strong employment relations, were involved in the design and delivery.
>
> Ten companies took part in the project. Each company nominated two "gatekeepers" to attend the programme and to act as the catalyst in developing and implementing workplace innovations. These gatekeepers participated in an initial short course of three and half days delivered over three months. This course gave the gatekeepers the opportunity to learn about good practice, develop their leadership skills, evaluate their own organisations with reference to workplace innovation practices, and formulate an action plan for change. A local further education provider was involved in delivering the course so that it could be accredited as Institute of Leadership and Management ILM Level 3 Award in Leadership and Management. Gatekeepers also took part in monthly half-day network meetings which provided greater depth of understanding in relation to specific aspects of workplace innovation, exploring practical dimensions of the initial course in more detail. Senior advisors from Acas served as "change facilitators, and provided in-company advice and guidance in relation to action plans.
>
> All the participating organisations reported that the Innovative Workplaces programme had led not only to the achievement of some of the workplace changes sought in their initial action plans but also to improvements in the wider employee relations climate. For the majority their aspirations for participation in the programme were achieved to a great extent and a range of different, but frequently related, organisational issues were addressed; these included improved levels of employee engagement, morale, communications between management and employees in different functional areas, workforce flexibility, and the implementation of change. Respondents from the smaller organisations were especially positive and more likely to have a shared view within the organisation about the outcomes of the programme and its business benefits. Additionally, an economic impact assessment reported an overall minimum return on investment of £ 4 for every £ 1 of public sector expenditure. Positive impacts were reported in terms of Gross Value Added per employee (including productivity gains) and jobs safeguarded or created. (See Chapter 4 of this publication for more information).
>
> Source: Tekes (2014), Liideri – Business, Productivity and Joy at Work; a new Finnish National Programme, *www.workplaceinnovation.org/nl/kennis/kennisbank/liideri---business--productivity-and-joy-at-work--a-new-finnish-national-programme/1235.*

Recommendation: Foster a stronger culture of entrepreneurship within employment services focused on the core working age population

Slovenia has set the goal of raising the youth entrepreneurial activity from 11% to at least the EU average of 12.8%. This is a welcome development and will be an important future source of new job creation opportunities and investments. Previous OECD research has highlighted the importance of the PES in making unemployed people aware of the opportunities to be gained from entrepreneurship (OECD, 2015). This rapid assessment also highlighted the importance of using ESF funding to highlight successful initiatives to inspire unemployed individuals.

Between 2007 and 2013, the PES delivered entrepreneurship opportunities through the self-employment programme, which provided subsidies to about 24 000 individuals. More than 85% of these participants survived the first two years, while 94% survived the first year. Moreover, 19% of self-employed also became employers and created more than 2 600 new jobs. The share of women was first aimed to be 40%, but on average it reached over 41% and was 45.2% is 2013.

The government should consider re-introducing this programme or launching a programme that focuses on core working age individuals and older workers. The previous OECD rapid policy assessment noted the narrow focus of current entrepreneurship programmes on highly educated unemployed youth. This is a critical age group but other efforts are also required to stimulate entrepreneurship within unemployed individuals outside of this demographic group. To overcome potential opposition from union groups, a consultation process could be launched to build awareness about the need for action in this area.

Being inclusive

Recommendation: Continue to leverage the role of the social enterprise sector in supporting inclusive growth

Slovenia performs relatively well in terms of inclusiveness compared to other OECD countries. For example, Slovenia has the lowest rate of income inequality post taxes and transfers of all OECD countries (OECD, 2015). Despite this performance, a number of significant challenges remain in integrating disadvantaged groups and migrants. In Slovenia, there is a strong history of division of labour along gender lines, and challenges with the integration of the Roma people, as well as immigrants (within the context of low overall flows of immigration,). Additionally, in addressing long-term unemployment, there are clear capacity gaps within the PES, as hiring freezes have left many of the psychologist and career counsellor positions unfilled when former staff have retired or left the organisation. Place-based disparities also exist – while Slovenia has a relatively low rate of regional disparities when measured by GDP per capita, the impact of the financial crisis was geographically concentrated, with more than half of all job losses occurring in only 2 of Slovenia's 12 regions (OECD, 2014c).

For Roma populations, sustained attention is needed to identify and implement measures that best stimulate their inclusion in education, employment, and training from an early age, while also improving their overall living conditions. In terms of addressing the division of labour along gender lines, lessons such as those learned from a successful project undertaken in Maribor to provide employer-based training for women in traditionally male-dominated professions could be more broadly shared.

Slovenia should continue to focus on the role of the social enterprise sector in reaching out to disadvantaged population. Previous OECD research found that Slovenia's specific economic and political history had resulted in an under-utilisation of the social enterprise sector (Spears et al., 2010). More recent reforms such as the introduction of a national Social Enterprise Act in 2011 represent important progress. However, within the case studies analysed for the purpose of this study, it appears that the current suite of programmes and funding are not optimal. Thus, continued attention should be paid to how the potential of this sector can be fulfilled.

References

The City of New York (2014), "Career Pathways: One City Working Together", www1.nyc.gov/assets/careerpathways/downloads/pdf/career-pathways-full-report.pdf.

The City of New York (2015), "Career Pathways: Progress Update", www1.nyc.gov/assets/careerpathways/downloads/pdf/Career-Pathways-Progress-Update.pdf; www.nyc.gov/html/ohcd/downloads/pdf/jobs_for_nyers_task_force_flyer.pdf.

Evans, S. and G. Bosch (2012), "Apprenticeships in London: Boosting Skills in a City Economy – With Comment on Lessons from Germany", OECD Local Economic and Employment Development (LEED) Working Papers, No. 2012/08, OECD Publishing, Paris, http://dx.doi.org/10.1787/5k9b9mjcxp35-en.

OECD (forthcoming, 2017b), OECD Economic Surveys: Slovenia 2017, OECD Publishing, Paris.

OECD/ILO (2017), Engaging Employers in Apprenticeship Opportunities, OECD Publishing, Paris, http://dx.doi.org/10.1787/9789264266681-en.

OECD (2016a), Getting Skills Right: Assessing and Anticipating Changing Skill Needs, OECD Publishing, Paris, http://dx.doi.org/10.1787/9789264252073-en.

OECD (2016b), Employment and Skills Strategies in Poland, OECD Publishing, Paris, http://dx.doi.org/10.1787/9789264256521-en

OECD (2016c), Job Creation and Local Economic Development 2016, OECD Publishing, Paris, http://dx.doi.org/10.1787/9789264261976-en.

OECD (2016d), OECD Employment Outlook 2016, OECD Publishing, Paris, http://dx.doi.org/10.1787/empl_outlook-2016-en.

OECD (2015), OECD Economic Surveys: Slovenia 2015, OECD Publishing, Paris, http://dx.doi.org/10.1787/eco_surveys-svn-2015-en.

OECD (2014a), Job Creation and Local Economic Development, OECD Publishing, Paris, http://dx.doi.org/10.1787/9789264215009-en.

OECD (2014b), Employment and Skills Strategies in Ireland, OECD Reviews on Local Job Creation, OECD Publishing, Paris, http://dx.doi.org/10.1787/9789264207912-en.

OECD (2014c), OECD Regional Outlook 2014: Regions and Cities: Where Policies and People Meet, OECD Publishing, Paris, http://dx.doi.org/10.1787/9789264201415-en.

Spear, R. et al. (2010), "Improving Social Inclusion at the Local Level through the Social Economy: Report for Slovenia", OECD Local Economic and Employment Development (LEED) Working Papers, No. 2010/16, OECD Publishing, Paris, .

Tekes (2014), "Liideri – Business, Productivity and Joy at Work: A new Finnish National Programme", www.workplaceinnovation.org/nl/kennis/kennisbank/liideri---business--productivity-and-joy-at-work--a-new-Finnish-national-programme/1235.

ORGANISATION FOR ECONOMIC CO-OPERATION AND DEVELOPMENT

The OECD is a unique forum where governments work together to address the economic, social and environmental challenges of globalisation. The OECD is also at the forefront of efforts to understand and to help governments respond to new developments and concerns, such as corporate governance, the information economy and the challenges of an ageing population. The Organisation provides a setting where governments can compare policy experiences, seek answers to common problems, identify good practice and work to co-ordinate domestic and international policies.

The OECD member countries are: Australia, Austria, Belgium, Canada, Chile, the Czech Republic, Denmark, Estonia, Finland, France, Germany, Greece, Hungary, Iceland, Ireland, Israel, Italy, Japan, Korea, Latvia, Luxembourg, Mexico, the Netherlands, New Zealand, Norway, Poland, Portugal, the Slovak Republic, Slovenia, Spain, Sweden, Switzerland, Turkey, the United Kingdom and the United States. The European Union takes part in the work of the OECD.

OECD Publishing disseminates widely the results of the Organisation's statistics gathering and research on economic, social and environmental issues, as well as the conventions, guidelines and standards agreed by its members.

www.ingramcontent.com/pod-product-compliance
Lightning Source LLC
Chambersburg PA
CBHW082351220526
45470CB00008B/2709